Other Books by Joseph Pluta

Economics:

From Human Evolution to Evolutionary Economics
A Micro View of Industry (with Hilal Yilmaz)
Human Progress Amid Resistance to Change
The Marginal Gospel
The Story of Economics
From Adam and Eve to Adam Smith
The Elusive Quest for Efficiency in an Inefficient World (with James Willis)
The Market: Mainstream and Evolutionary Views
Consumers, Competition, and Corporations
Regional Change in the U. S. Brewing Industry
The Imperfect Microscope (with James Willis and Michael Fabritius)
Small Trees in the Large Forest
The Art of Making Choices (with James Willis and Martin Primack)
Markets, Merchants, and Monopolies (with James Willis)
The Energy Picture: Problems and Prospects
Microeconomic Horizons (with James Willis and Martin Primack)
Explorations in Microeconomics (with James Willis and Martin Primack)
Economic and Business Issues of the 1980s

Fiction:

Whatever Happened to Our Dreams?
21 Yesterdays
Small Town Michigan Tales
Two Peninsulas

An Evolutionary Alternative to Mainstream Microeconomics

Joseph E. Pluta

CreateSpace Publishing
North Charleston, South Carolina

Printed in the United States of America

ISBN - 13: 9781519290953
ISBN - 10: 1519290950

webpage: josephepluta.com

If a million people say a foolish thing,

it is still a foolish thing

Anatole France

The only function of economic forecasting is to

make astrology look respectable

John Kenneth Galbraith

One of the saddest lessons of history is this: if

we've been bamboozled long enough, we tend

to reject any evidence of the bamboozle

Carl Sagan

TABLE OF CONTENTS

Preface

For those who wish to study economic and social problems, there is no shortage of subject matter. Corporate scandals, banking crises, a disappearing middle class, growing job insecurity, global warming, and other serious concerns are more than abundant. Among the thousands of American economists, how many have investigated these or other similarly worthwhile topics? Surprisingly, the percentage is relatively small. Most have devoted their primary attention elsewhere.

As has been the case for some time, graduate programs in economics continue to emphasize analytical technique. On the whole, their models are impressive, mathematically sophisticated, and the culmination of ample scholarly effort.

Unfortunately, many such replicas of the economy are also unrealistic. Most do not address issues such as those listed above or contribute to problem solving generally. Particularly suspect are their assumptions which often do not even vaguely resemble the world they purport to explain. Without these convenient simplifying conjectures, the models do not and will not work.

Some examples include the following. Consumers always behave rationally. People pursuing their own self interest automatically make others better off as well. Business efficiency increases the more closely firms approximate standards consistent with something called pure competition. Wages paid to employees and managers are based on how much each contributes to output or revenue. A number of economic laws hold true in all times and places.

Under contrived conditions like these, if all participants in the economy maximize or minimize something when required to do so, quantitatively precise results will occur. With minimal interference in these assumed behavior patterns, the outcomes will be logical and optimal for all concerned.

The quest for greater precision and rigor has presumably been undertaken in an effort to attain a stature comparable to the respect enjoyed by the physical sciences. What began as seemingly harmless "physics envy" has instead produced a great amount of mental masturbation and fictitious wishful thinking.

To be sure, there are model builders today whose work has drawn the attention of corporations and government agencies seeking economic forecasts. The resulting predictions have often been far less accurate than advertised and promised. Doctoring assumptions to make results conform more closely to what a given audience wants the forecast to say is a temptation that has not always been resisted.

A relatively small group of economists has taken a series of different approaches that more directly address difficult problems. This school of thought is known by two interchangeable names: *evolutionary economics* and *institutional economics*. Their inspiration may be traced to many sources, the most prominent of which are the writings of Thorstein Veblen, John R. Commons, Wesley C. Mitchell, Clarence E. Ayres, Gunnar Myrdal, John Kenneth Galbraith, Kenneth Boulding, and a number of more recent scholars including several contemporaries.

This group identifies the problems listed above and others as complex and multifaceted. It recognizes that comprehension and analysis require methods that are broad in scope and capable of change when circumstances warrant. Its members are willing to engage in experimentation. They welcome imprecision because the world is imprecise. They believe in the importance of history and acceptance of change while acknowledging that change is often resisted. They seek to widen rather than narrow the focus of their research. They have little or no use for hidden political agendas disguised as value free, objective analysis.

This book is about some of the approaches and applications of evolutionary economics. Its common ground with earlier work in this field is dissent against views and methods that have gained wide acceptance and have become the mainstream of the profession.

In the pages that follow, many of these widely accepted methods are briefly reviewed before their individual shortcomings are discussed. Where appropriate, alternatives are offered and suggestions for new directions in economic thinking are given. These alternatives are more inclusive of yet to be modeled variables, more interdisciplinary, more realistic, and arguably more interesting.

Some evolutionary economists understandably might prefer a different approach or combination of approaches. Especially during the early to mid twentieth century, the University of Wisconsin, Columbia University, and other reputable institutions produced significant scholarship with an evolutionary emphasis. This combined body of work is hereby acknowledged with appreciation for its influence on contemporary scholars.

My own educational experiences include the privilege of having been a student of Ayres at the conclusion of his career at the University of Texas. While insights from a number of evolutionary economists may be found in this book, its primary focus stems from the scholarship of Ayres and from his recollections of conversations with Veblen.

The book is intended for the general audience. No similar survey of the subject currently exists. Before retiring, I used drafts of the chapters in three different undergraduate courses: evolutionary economics, history of economic thought, and microeconomic principles. In order to present dissenting views of mainstream concepts, the current alignment of chapters is organized to parallel the sequence of topics in a microeconomics course. During my final ten years in the classroom, I taught multiple sections of micro principles that compared mainstream and evolutionary perspectives. I have found students and colleagues quite receptive to this comparative approach.

The challenges in presenting "the" evolutionary point of view on any single topic are numerous. After a thorough review of existing literature, I have attempted to represent each position taken as accurately as possible. It is my hope that those who read these chapters may become more aware of deficiencies inherent in the neoclassical gospel. Portions of this book have previously appeared under the title *Human Progress Amid Resistance to Change* published by Friesen Press of Victoria, British Columbia and copyrighted under my name. Substantial updating and rewriting has occurred before the present book has gone to press.

My sincere thanks go to those evolutionary economists with whom I have had several conversations over the years. Their insights have taught me much about this perceptive yet far too often overlooked school of thought. This group includes Wendell Gordon, Kenneth Boulding, Charles Leathers, James Peach, William Dugger, Ray Marshall, Warren Samuels, Clifton Grubbs, Edythe Miller, and Lewis Hill. Many others (especially John Kenneth Galbraith, Gunnar Myrdal, Rick Tilman, and Malcolm Rutherford) have influenced me through their numerous books and professional articles.

Any errors contained herein are mine alone.

Joseph E. Pluta
Austin, Texas
December 2015

Chapter One

Mathematically Precise Fairy Tales

Mathematics brought rigor to economics.
Unfortunately, it also brought mortis.

Kenneth E. Boulding

Too large a proportion of recent 'mathematical' economics are mere concoctions.....in a maze of pretentious and unhelpful symbols.

John Maynard Keynes

The discipline of economics has yet to get over its childish passion for mathematics……at the expense of historical research and collaboration with the other social sciences.

Thomas Piketty

With the passage of time, a relatively large group of economists has come to accept some ideas and concepts more than others. For want of a better term, this group might be called the *mainstream.* Its dominance of the profession has influenced economic thinking at least since the nineteenth and maybe even the late eighteenth century. Those who studied the economy during the earlier of these two periods eventually came to be known as *classical economists.* In the following century, when their original ideas were more concisely defined and more neatly packaged, the heirs to this intellectual heritage eventually became known as *neoclassical economists.* Throughout this book, *mainstream and neoclassical economics will be considered to be one and the same.*

The Smith to Marshall Connection

The mainstream of the profession traces its roots to the philosophy of Adam Smith (1723-1790) who is often considered to be the "Father of Economics".[1] His impressive book, *The Wealth of Nations*, published in 1776, set forth a number of important concepts that defined the direction the newly emerging discipline was to take. Many of the ideas of Smith and other classical economists were refined and made more precise by a later generation of economists whose principal figure was Alfred Marshall (1842-1924).[2] His *Principles of Economics* was published in 1890 and achieved its maximum circulation forty years later. Marshall and his followers sought to make the discipline more scientific, more analytical, and more quantitative. Their imprint on the profession can still be seen today in the ideas and work of the mainstream. The general approaches of Smith and Marshall were sufficiently similar that they can be considered part of the same intellectual tradition.

Smith emphasized such now well-known concepts as the division of labor, the invisible hand, economic growth, consumer sovereignty, and a streamlined role for government compared to what had existed during the two centuries prior to his birth. Classical concepts of how interest rates, prices, and wages were determined all emphasized that government tampering with such mechanisms was unnecessary and potentially harmful. The classical economists also believed that prolonged unemployment was an impossibility and that, if interest rates, prices, and wages were allowed to fluctuate freely, full employment would be quickly and neatly restored. Such beliefs were dealt a crushing blow during the Great Depression of the 1930s but until then remained an unchallenged mantra of the classical and neoclassical schools of thought.

The Wealth of Nations was specifically targeted at the

economic philosophy of mercantilism and its notions of the role of government and of money. After the collapse of feudalism in Europe at the time of the Renaissance, the early merchant capitalists advocated strong central government direction of the economy and believed that nations became wealthy by stockpiling gold and silver. In particular, mercantilist inspired European leaders championed the limitation of imports, the maintenance of tightly controlled overseas colonies, and even piracy on the high seas in order to insure that precious metals flowed into the mother country. Smith believed that the inflow of specie without increasing the production of goods was likely to cause only inflation, as more money in circulation bid up the prices of a given supply of products.

Rather than hoarding precious metals, a nation became wealthy, Smith argued, by increasing its ability to produce real things. The Industrial Revolution of the 18th century demonstrated this rather clearly. Therefore, Smith and his disciples emphasized those factors responsible for economic growth. Technology, natural resources, new machines in the workplace, along with an abundant and well-trained workforce contributed much more to prosperity than gold and silver did. Economic growth potentially benefitted wide segments of the population as business owners prosper, workers receive higher wages and encounter more job opportunities, and consumers face a growing availability of heretofore scarce products.

Smith used the metaphor of the *invisible hand* to allege the widespread benefit of self-interest. He believed the unseen hand of competition regulated the economy much better than the strong, visible hand of mercantilist government. According to this metaphor, each individual pursuing his or her own self-interest automatically guaranteed that the public good was served. To enhance their own economic well being by producing goods that people needed, producers were made better off while consumers were as well. This tied in nicely with *consumer sovereignty*, the notion that the consumer was king. Those businesses that produced what consumers wanted were successful while those that did not were not. The consumer, in other words, allegedly called the shots.

One of Smith's followers, Jeremy Bentham (1748-1832), argued that consumers sought to maximize satisfaction in their purchases. Each buying decision was presumably made after rational calculation of the benefits and costs associated with a given product compared to other products. Frivolous spur of the moment impulse buying was ruled out by assumption. This notion of *consumer rationality* was controversial from the beginning and has remained so to the present day.

Measuring happiness, pleasure, or satisfaction was not an easy task. To sidestep the issue, Bentham invented the concept of *utility,* or want-satisfying power. Utility was a characteristic supposedly possessed by all goods. The total amount of satisfaction received by consuming a good was called *total utility.* The additional amount of satisfaction or utility received by consuming additional amounts of a good was called *marginal utility.*

Bentham argued that all goods were subject to the *principle of diminishing marginal utility.* This meant that the more of a good one consumed, the smaller the additional satisfaction derived from each consecutive unit. On a hot day, the first can of Coke is wonderful, the second is still great, the third pretty good, and the fourth only so-so. Goods such as ice cream cones, glasses of beer, and even money are allegedly subject to this principle. Each successive unit consumed adds smaller and smaller amounts to total utility.

There have always been issues about whether this utility or satisfaction can be measured, whether one person's utility can be precisely compared to another's, and even if consumers in reality behaved this way. Nevertheless, some of Marshall's associates built upon Bentham's original thinking on these matters. These early theories of consumer behavior still influence the way many, if not most, mainstream economists view the consumer today.

The neoclassical interpretation of Bentham, however, differed in some respects from his original views. Both agreed that additional utility received from having more and more of an item diminished. Bentham used this idea to justify government redistribution of income from the rich to the poor. Since a dollar taken from a rich man reduced that person's utility by only a small amount but added much more additional utility to a poor man when given to him, such redistribution made sense in his view.

Neoclassicals were not so inclined. Instead, they used the idea of *diminishing marginal utility* to explain their *law of demand.* If consuming large quantities of a good added smaller and smaller amounts to total utility, the only way a business could get people to buy more of its products was to lower the price. Therefore, neoclassicals reasoned, price and quantity demanded are inversely related. At higher prices, people would buy less but, at lower prices, people would buy more. The neoclassical economists then attempted to quantify the specific price-quantity relationship for individual products.

Another "diminishing" concept concerned with laborers and the output they produce was developed during the classical period. David Ricardo (1772-1823) first advanced this idea to explain how *increases* in agricultural output like wheat or corn get smaller as more and more workers are added to a given plot of land or as more land is added to existing farms. With limited acreage in England (then and now), the situation is made even worse because the most fertile land is cultivated first. When more food is needed, farmers must begin using their less fertile or lower quality land. Higher demand for food, however, is forcing food prices upward.

When he became a member of the British Parliament, Ricardo used this *diminishing returns* principle to argue for repeal of special interest tariffs on food imports. Such legislation benefitted owners of land by keeping domestic food prices high to the detriment of those who worked on the land and had to pay higher prices for the food they produced.

Later economists in the neoclassical period, especially the American John Bates Clark (1847-1938), used this same concept to argue that everyone was paid exactly what they deserve, labor was not exploited, and the distribution of income between rich and poor was precisely as it should be. Clark and others believed that workers were paid based on the amount each contributed to the business firm's output. According to this theory, workers who are more productive deserve better pay than those who are less productive, certainly an argument that is not unreasonable. The fact that precise measurement of the difference often proved to be difficult was once again downplayed by those who supported the principle. When fifty workers are employed on an automobile assembly line, for example, is it really possible to measure how many additional cars any one worker contributed to total output?

Mainstream economists today use concepts like diminishing returns in an attempt to measure worker productivity and to determine the best mix of workers, machines, and other resources in the workplace. Especially in large corporations, identifying the optimal mix of resources can reduce costs and make firms more profitable. Most business decisions are marginal decisions. They involve reasoning at the margin. Should the firm hire a few more workers or a few more machines? Should it hire more of one and less of another? Should it raise prices by a few cents or lower them by a few cents?

Marginal here does not imply unimportant. Instead, marginal refers to small changes that can be extremely important for the survivability and profitability of the firm. The neoclassical economists specialized in developing these marginal concepts and in making marginal reasoning a central part of the profession. For this reason, they were initially called *marginalists* and their work during the nineteenth century was sometimes referred to as the marginalist revolution. Whether a genuine revolution or not, economists in the neoclassical tradition still maintain that marginal reasoning continues to guide business and consumer decision making.

Marshall brought the concepts of supply and demand together and argued that price was determined at the point where the two were equal or curves representing each crossed on a graph. He based this analysis and others on the concept of *equilibrium*, a position toward which economic forces gravitate. The notion was borrowed from the physical sciences including astronomy, where a balancing of forces explains how planets maintain their orbits and do not collide. It did not take long before human behavior was explained using the same idea. A consumer was judged to be in equilibrium when he or she maximized utility subject to a budget constraint. A business achieved equilibrium when it maximized profit or perhaps maximized revenue or maybe even minimized cost. Of course, a given market was in equilibrium when the forces of supply and demand just balanced each other.

Calculus is a mathematical tool that enables fairly easy identification of maximum and minimum values. This technique was applied in the realm of economics to suggest that people and business firms should logically behave as maximizers and minimizers. Neoclassical economists, therefore, attempted to devise mathematically precise economic laws that held true in all places and at all times much like laws in physical science. Just as physics had its law of gravity and its law of thermodynamics, economics now had its laws of supply and demand as well as its laws of diminishing returns and diminishing marginal utility.

Marshall's *Principles* used these and other laws along with concepts like the representative firm and ideal competition to set the stage for later development of the discipline. To gain an appreciation for the contribution of Marshall, open a copy of any contemporary economics text. Several of the chapters dealing with microeconomics, especially their graphics, are still based largely on the work of Marshall. No similar claim can be made about any other nineteenth century economist.

Marshall was optimistic about what the forces of competition could accomplish. He argued that, as small firms grew, they became more efficient. Mass production on assembly lines, more thorough division of labor, greater use of technology, and more specialized management skills all contributed to lower costs of production. Larger more established firms could also obtain lower interest rates on loans.

If bigger is better, if more efficient firms naturally grow in size, and if less efficient firms do not survive, some would argue the eventual and inevitable result is either *monopoly* (one firm) or, only slightly better, maybe only a few firms. When this happens, competition either vanishes or little of it is left. With fewer choices, consumers suffer. Here is where Marshall's optimism provides an argument that this negative outcome will not occur.

Marshall believed that, encouraged by high profit levels, new firms would enter the industry before all the benefits of large size would be realized. Ingenious entrepreneurs would bring new ideas to make their firms even more efficient than long established firms and their aging leaders. Marshall also reasoned that business owners would not live forever. As they advanced in years, their firms would also age and subsequently either die with them or struggle under less experienced and less hungry management.

This line of thought was made possible because of Marshall's assumption that this all begins with a "representative firm". As the modern corporation emerged, however, near monopoly firms did dominate the market and, because of multiple owners of corporate stock, did not die.

By the early twentieth century, most economists still structured their thinking about industries on models of competition and monopoly. Under competition, there were many firms; under monopoly, there was only one. With the emergence of giant corporations in the 1890s and their central role in the economy by the 1920s, this twofold division was clearly inadequate. Several industries were dominated by a small number of very large firms. Others had numerous relatively small firms whose characteristics were still quite different from the ideal type of competition outlined by Marshall.

More Recent Refinements

Needed were models to describe the vast array of businesses that lay between the extremes of ideal competition and monopoly. In 1933, two researchers working independently on opposite sides of the Atlantic published their remarkably similar findings. Both were in the neoclassical tradition even though both were also heavily influenced by other schools of thought. Edward Chamberlin[3] of Harvard University called his soon to be classic *The Theory of Monopolistic Competition.* One of Marshall's students, Joan Robinson[4] of Cambridge University, entitled her similarly impressive work *The Economics of Imperfect Competition.*

Significant features of both books, which describe the case of less than perfect competition among relatively small firms, continue to appear in economics textbooks today. One of the issues that Chamberlin and Robinson addressed was the economics of advertising, an industry that by the 1920s had come of age. Even advertising can be subjected to marginal analysis. When a firm, for example, spends an additional million dollars to advertise its product, does this action result in sales increasing by more than a million dollars?

Several models of corporate giants have been developed throughout the twentieth century. These include game theory, the cartel, dominant firm price leadership, price rigidity, cost-plus pricing, and several others. These models attempt to explain a market setting called *oligopoly* where there are only a small number of large firms in an industry. Although credit for originating the term has been given to several 19th and 20th century economists, oligopoly is discussed somewhat earlier in Thomas More's fictional *Utopia*, published in 1516.[5]

Increasingly popular today, *game theory* is a strategy of decision making under uncertainty similar to a game like poker or chess. How one plays the game depends on what a rival does. If one firm lowers prices or advertises more, rival firms must decide how they will respond so as not to lose customers. A *cartel* is a formal written agreement that divides the market, fixes prices, allows rival firms to agree not to compete, and enables them to behave like a monopoly. Because of its anti-competitive features, the cartel is illegal in interstate commerce in the U. S. OPEC is a cartel in the global market while professional sports provide a good example domestically. The former is not subject to American antitrust law while the latter has been granted an exemption.

Dominant-firm price leadership is a strategy in which a large firm sets prices that smaller firms in the industry follow. In the past, both U. S. Steel and General Motors have behaved as price leaders. *Price rigidity* is the tendency in some markets for prices to remain unchanged for fairly long periods of time because all firms have similar market shares and any price change by one would reduce its revenue from sales. Household appliances, including TVs, are possible examples. *Cost-plus pricing* is a strategy where a firm estimates its cost per unit and adds a percentage markup of profit to determine price. Many firms likely set prices in this manner.

Mainstream economists today argue that all of these models are useful in describing *some* features of decision making in large firms. Even they admit, however, that this remains an area where much work needs to be done. The most promising area of recent research involves game theory whose methods are being applied to a wider range of economic issues than has previously been the case.

Finally, mainstream techniques are applied not only to the strategies of both consumers and business firms but also to analysis of government policies. When markets fail to deliver products efficiently, government frequently intervenes in an effort to alleviate the problem. Pollution is one example while some portions of health care and education are others. Private business, on its own, has clearly failed to address all three issues adequately. Some government programs work better than others. Mainstream microeconomics can be used to evaluate the efficiency of such government efforts.

A technique called *benefit cost analysis* is increasingly being used to evaluate government programs at federal, state, and local levels. By comparing benefits to costs, it can be determined if a program should be undertaken and what level of resources should be devoted to specific activities. Such analysis constitutes yet another example of reasoning at the margin. Does an additional dollar of cost to the taxpayer contribute more than an additional dollar of benefit in a given government program such as national defense, flood control, or environmental protection? Those techniques used to evaluate private business firm performance are adapted for similar evaluation purposes in the government sector. Mainstream economists argue that use of such methods provides better information on which managers in government agencies can make decisions.

Practical applications of mainstream methods have mostly come during the second half of the twentieth century. The early neoclassical economists, whose contributions Marshall neatly synthesized while adding much of his own analysis, were not primarily interested in developing the discipline along lines that would provide assistance to policy makers. They also did not focus on offering explanations of important economic trends that were actually occurring during their day.

Especially puzzling is the fact that, despite the fairly large number of economists who hailed from Britain, none of them devoted serious study to the decline in British economic global influence as evidenced by falling exports and a less dynamic overall economy.[6] Instead, their primary motivation was establishing timeless economic laws consistent with similar principles advanced in the physical sciences.

During the early 19th century, many educated professionals were still widely read in a number of different disciplines. Academic specialization, to be sure, already existed but scholars in one field were far more cognizant of at least major principles in other fields than is often the case today. In fact, methods used in other disciplines were often likely candidates for adaptation elsewhere. Economists at this time were more impressed with what was occurring in physics, chemistry, astronomy, and mathematics than in history, psychology, anthropology, and biology.

Several of the neoclassicals, including Marshall, were quite well versed in mathematics and the principles they advanced cried out for proof that could be found in actual tests of these numerical relationships. During the 1920s, a branch of economics called *econometrics* emerged and provided the methodology to conduct such tests using actual statistical data that were increasingly becoming available. As technology, including the computer, has advanced, econometric models have become more complex and have evolved into the standard methodology used by the mainstream of the profession. Over time, a larger number of corporations have hired economists trained in the latest econometric techniques to estimate demand for their products and offer other economic forecasts. Some government agencies have engaged in similar hiring practices.

Use of a more advanced analytical apparatus may be seen as a logical outcome of early work done by neoclassical economists. They were the ones who provided the direction for, and who suggested the necessity of, determining more precisely how two economic variables, for example, were in fact related. Many of the people drawn to the study of mainstream methods today are more likely to come from backgrounds in engineering, physics, and mathematics than from various social sciences.

What the economics profession today has most in common with the profession in Marshall's time is that it is not centered on current economic problems but rather is organized around a kit of tools. Current issues begging for economic analysis include recurring crises in the world of finance, consequences of global warming, and the effects of outsourcing manufacturing jobs to China and elsewhere. Instead, mainstream research energies, using differential calculus and even more advanced mathematics under highly unrealistic assumptions about consumer and managerial behavior, have been diverted to more theoretical pursuits. In the extreme, some research has even addressed how closely a given situation approximates long run equilibrium under a fictional concept like pure competition.

Conclusion

Smith's insightful description of the economic growth process inspired later generations of economists to assemble data that have largely supported this aspect of his work. The invisible hand metaphor, however, has been repeated over and over again without any verification of its claim. This particular fairy tale, therefore, has lacked even the most basic quantification, let alone any degree of mathematical precision.

Bentham's theory of consumer behavior is based on a concept, utility, that cannot possibly be measured. And yet, his many followers have tried either to do so or to devise graphical methods that enable claims of one bundle of goods outranking another in consumer bliss without saying by how much. With calculus, one could even pull a hypothetical function out of thin air and *maximize it* even though actual quantification of what was being measured was impossible! This was fairy tale making at its finest. It represents not only a more than century long waste of time but its indoctrination of millions of students in its unsubstantiated accuracy and alleged importance would border on child abuse if college students were just a few years younger.

The claim by neoclassical economists that each and every worker is paid exactly what they deserve is yet another fiction that has gained widespread appeal. The notion that a worker should be compensated based on what he or she contributes makes perfect sense. The fact that precise contributions of individuals can rarely be measured, however, makes the principle somewhat less applicable. In this case, there is an assumed ability to calculate that does not exist.

The "law" of demand, the "law" of diminishing marginal utility, the "law" of diminishing returns, and other such inventions *are not laws at all*. They were never passed by a U. S. Congress or British Parliament and signed into law by a president or prime minister. More importantly, they were never proven the way laws in physics have been verified over and over again. If you drop a pencil a thousand times, it will fall to the floor exactly one thousand times. That is the *law* of gravity. As will be demonstrated in detail later, there are exceptions to all of the above "laws" in economics. These concepts were merely *declared* to be laws by overzealous neoclassical economists who wanted to make their discipline look more like the physical sciences. Because of their collective inferiority complex and desire to ape the analytically more impressive disciplines of physics and astronomy, these ideas have been misnamed and oversold to multiple successive generations of students.

For more than a century, mainstream microeconomics has sought more precision, more sophisticated analytical techniques, and more ways to make economics more scientific. Following the mainstream lead, the discipline today uses extensive graphical analysis and increasingly complex mathematical models. While nineteenth century neoclassical economists clearly narrowed the focus of the discipline, the mainstream today is applying its analytical tools to updated models of business firms and government. Theories of monopolistic competition, oligopoly, and benefit cost analysis as well as methods of business forecasting have all been developed since the time of Marshall. How effective has the research of this more recent mainstream group become?

One of the major current debates both within and outside the economics profession concerns the effectiveness and practical applicability of the discipline's more rigorous methods.[7] Have they genuinely enhanced our understanding of economic relationships? Have they provided useful information to decision makers in business and in government so that better strategies can be pursued? Have they made the tasks of those who formulate economic policies that affect millions of people easier or more difficult? Have economic forecasts of future events become more accurate or less so?

And perhaps most importantly, has the increased "mathematization" of the discipline encouraged more interest in it? Or has this pursuit of precise quantification merely created an elite group of highly skilled technicians who are communicating mainly with each other by playing high level mind games?

Not surprisingly, dissenting points of view have also influenced the focus and methods of the discipline. These will be addressed in the following chapter.

Footnotes:

1. The literature on Adam Smith is substantial and several readable biographies exist. See, for example, Samuel Hollander, *The Economics of Adam Smith,* (Toronto: University of Toronto Press, 1973) and Mark Blaug, ed., *Adam Smith,* (Brookfield, VT: Edward Elgar, 1991).

2. Peter Groenenwegen, *A Soaring Eagle: Alfred Marshall, 1842–1924,* (Brookfield, VT: Edward Elgar, 1995). This nearly 900 page work is *the* authoritative biography on the life and contributions of Marshall. For more recent perspectives, see: Patrik Aspers, "Alfred Marshall and the Concept of Class", *American Journal of Economics and Sociology,* 69, 1 (January 2010), pp. 151-165 and Jaques Kerstenetzky, "Alfred Marshall on Big Business", *Cambridge Journal of Economics*, 34, 3 (May 2010), pp. 569-586.

3. Believing his work to be more advanced than that of Joan Robinson, Chamberlin devoted substantial effort to proving his claim but was largely unsuccessful in doing so. See Nahid Aslanbeigui and Guy Oakes, "Hostage to Fortune: Edward Chamberlin and the Reception of *The Theory of Monopolistic Competition*", *History of Political Economy*, 43, 3 (Fall 2011), pp. 471-512.

4. Some of the ideas found in this classic work were actually introduced the previous year. See Joan Robinson, "Imperfect Competition and Falling Supply Price", *Economic Journal*, 42, 168 (December 1932), pp. 544-554.

5. Joseph A. Schumpeter, *A History of Economic Analysis,* (London: Allen and Unwin, 1954), p. 208.

6. John Mills, *A Critical History of Economics,* (New York: Palgrave Macmillan, 2003), p. 120.

7. Daniel Sutter, "The Market, the Firm, and the Economics Profession", *American Journal of Economics and Sociology*, 68, 5 (November 2009), pp. 1041-1061.

Chapter Two

Knowledge and Habitual Behavior

A man who uses an imaginary map thinking that it is a true one is likely to be worse off than someone with no map at all.

E. F. Schumacher

New ideas are difficult just because they are new. Repetition has somehow plastered over the gaps and inconsistencies in the old ones, and the new cannot penetrate.

Joan Robinson

If the misery of the poor be caused, not by the laws of nature, but by our institutions, great is our sin.

Charles Darwin

What Veblen said in effect was: The hell with the whole business of price theory; it is meaningless.

Clarence E. Ayres

Harriet Martineau, whose circle of friends included two prominent classical economists, Thomas Malthus and John Stuart Mill, was a nineteenth century English writer who is often considered to be the first woman sociologist. Paul Samuelson, the first American to win the Nobel Prize in Economics (1970) and a strong defender of mainstream economics, once stated that Harriet Martineau "made fairy tales out of economics" while modern economists "make economics out of fairy tales".[1] His casual, partially tongue in cheek, observation might be worth a closer look.

Our culture is openly fond of its traditions, myths, and

legends. Santa Claus, the Easter Bunny, the Tooth Fairy, animated superheroes, mermaids, leprechauns, and invented deities are among our favorite, even beloved, fictional characters. When kept in perspective, these icons are sometimes entertaining and generally harmless. If an important business or personal career decision has to be made, most of us would look elsewhere for guidance.

The always-rational consumer, the perfectly competitive business, and the timeless economic law are also fantasies. Around this triumvirate of imaginative folklore, however, an entire discipline has been assembled and taught as if it were absolute truth. In this case, the potential consequences are anything but harmless. If a premise is contradicted by fact, how beneficial could actions based on such a premise possibly be? The discipline's policy recommendations aim to influence the behavior of individual consumers, the goals of businesses, and the programs of governments. A cleverly concocted and masterfully delivered message may glow in its popular appeal but it is unlikely to shed much light on economic reality. And yet, the sales pitch has captivated a profession whose only serious question seems to be how to measure these and other artificial creations more precisely.

The discipline in question is called *mainstream economics.* When based on these fabrications, its focus is often misleading in describing something as important, *and real,* as the economy. Some of us might find it convenient to accept the premises on which one or more of this trio of fantasies is based. Decision-making would be easier, for example, if certain laws could be invoked at any time the way some people find comfort in catchy slogans or popular clichés. If these laws are not always valid, however, they are about as useful as cute sayings or the advice of a leprechaun.

Many mainstream economists recognize the shaky foundation upon which their methods are based but that has rarely discouraged them from building analytical models that appear to be scientific. In order to "think like an economist," most students today are asked to accept these and other *assumptions* so that they can become more adept at using the analytical tools. Over the past several decades, this approach has achieved near legendary status as the dominant and, in the eyes of some, the *only* path to economic competence.

The Importance of History

Contrary to popular myth, there are many possible approaches to studying economics. The discipline has evolved over several centuries in response to specific economic and social problems across the globe. In many cases, when crises surfaced, they were vastly different from anything then known. A previously decreed economic law would have been of little value in addressing a new crisis. Instead, proposed solutions were often heavily debated with input from groups of people who possessed conflicting interests in the outcome. As a result, various schools of thought have contributed to a constantly changing body of knowledge that, therefore, must be viewed as a continually evolving process. Understanding how and why economics has altered its focus over time is crucial in knowing how it got to where it is now.

Briefly and bluntly stated, history is important. Few, if any, economic principles are genuinely timeless. There are exceptions to every self-proclaimed economic "law" and no such law is valid at all times and in all places. With sincere apologies to popular legend, some things "just aren't so". In place of the mainstream disdain for, and frequently exhibited ignorance of, history, knowledge of key events in world economic history and the history of economic thought are essential in providing a more complete picture of the discipline's relevance. The emergence of neoclassical economics was merely one chapter in that history.

Critique of the Mainstream

Despite its wide acceptance, the mainstream has always had its critics who have also drawn a sympathetic and sizable following. Several schools of thought that dissented from mainstream positions have offered valuable insights and devastating critiques. One school will receive particular attention in this book, primarily because its methods adapt well to changing circumstances and its critique is becoming increasingly relevant today. This broad dissent has come to be known as *evolutionary economics.* Because much of its focus is on institutions, that is, groupings of people with common behavior patterns, members of this group are also frequently called *institutionalists* or institutional economists. Throughout this book, *evolutionary economics and institutionalism will be considered one and the same.*

Evolutionary economics is a dissent against a number of the principles popularized by Smith, Marshall, and their followers. It argues that, at best, the mainstream gives an incomplete picture and, at worst, a highly inaccurate one. Its reluctant founder, Thorstein Veblen (1857-1929), argued for a more broadly based economics that paid closer attention to principles advanced in other disciplines.[2] He rejected the idea of building a discipline on a metaphor like the invisible hand that was merely asserted and never proven. Ethically dubious and sometimes outright illegal practices of late 19th century corporations proved to Veblen that, by pursuing their own self-interest, such entities were automatically guaranteeing *only* their self-interest, at the direct expense of everyone else.

While publicly singing the praises of competition and limited government, corporate leaders in Veblen's day did whatever they could to eliminate competition in pursuit of monopoly power while benefitting from federal government favors, both financial and otherwise. The closer such firms got to becoming monopolies, the more they were able to withhold their output from the market in order to charge a higher price for it. Veblen called this artificially contrived scarcity *industrial sabotage*. Its practice, he warned, meant that making money and making goods could sometimes be distinctly different business strategies capable of producing vastly different results.

An Evolutionary Framework

Veblen also argued that the satisfaction maximizing consumers of mainstream economics were based on theories of human behavior that had long since been discredited by the psychology profession. People were not always rational, he maintained, and did not always make purchases based on hard calculations of how much they contributed to human pleasure, as the person who bought things on impulse amply demonstrated. In place of such a human caricature, Veblen drew upon advances made in Freudian psychology that said human beings behave according to underlying traits or motivational forces called *instincts*.

Such instincts, he argued, involved conscious effort toward some purposeful end result. While many existed, he focused primarily on four such instincts. The *parental bent* is a concern for family and others, broadly speaking, the human race. The *instinct of workmanship* is the pride one takes in ones work, the satisfaction one feels when creating something of quality, and the admiration one has for the skills of others. *Idle curiosity* is the quest for knowledge simply for the sake of knowing, not because of the financial reward that specific knowledge might bring. The *acquisitive drive*, or pursuit of profit, negates the parental bent because it is solely self-seeking and is not motivated by a desire to address the needs of the human family. To Veblen, throughout history the first three instincts worked together and contributed to human progress while being restrained and opposed by the institutions and traditions that the fourth instinct and others like it created.

Suggested Alternative Approaches

One of Veblen's students, Clarence Ayres (1891-1972), deciphered some of his teacher's obscure prose to formulate what has become an important part of evolutionary economic theory. To Veblen and Ayres, all societies and cultures have been influenced by two opposing forces. The first is *technology*, which is defined broadly as *tools plus human knowledge*. This force is dynamic, progressive, accepting of change, cumulative (one invention leads to another), continuous, and forward looking. It is the primary force in economic growth and human progress. It is the result, not of the profit motive, but of the combined effect of the parental bent, instinct of workmanship, and idle curiosity.

The second force has been called both *institutions* and *ceremonialism*. Institutions may be defined as groupings of people with similar behavior patterns. Ceremonialism is concerned with strict attention to prescribed procedures and established ways of doing things. This second force is static, past-binding, resistant to change, authoritative, and past-glorifying. It includes all customs, habits, myths, rituals, traditions, mores, taboos, and superstitions that result in conformity of behavior.[3]

To contemporary evolutionary economists, a "model" of this sort is far more valuable than anything devised by the mainstream. Over time, this approach has come to be known as the *Veblen-Ayres dichotomy*.[4] It will be used in this book to evaluate selected situations where its conflicting forces are most in evidence.

A harsh reality of human existence is that many of the issues that economists and others study are controversial. Clearly, therefore, more than one view must be considered in describing these issues. Over the years, the mainstream has sought more precision in its descriptions. As a result, it has narrowed its scope and become more analytical as well as more quantitative. Its models have abstracted from reality in search of establishing economic laws that possess some predictive power. In abstraction, some variables are omitted. The difficulty lies in choosing what is more important and eliminating what is less important. Sophisticated techniques of statistical inference have been devised to aid in this selection process. The mainstream or neoclassical approach alleges much success in its methods and results.

Evolutionary economists, by contrast, argue that the largely static models of the mainstream are inadequate for analyzing a world that is constantly changing. Despite being mathematically impressive, these models leave out much of what needs to be described and do not even ask important questions that need to be asked. Evolutionary economics rejects the claim that economic laws hold true for all time and instead seeks to broaden rather than narrow the focus of economics. It emphasizes the need for interdisciplinary inquiry, since actual problems and issues do not cooperate by neatly confining themselves to the boundaries of any single discipline. It argues that the mainstream record has not been impressive in either describing or predicting accurately.

Evolutionary economics proposes and advances a more dynamic approach to studying economies and the societies in which they operate.[5] Such recent topics as the wave of corporate scandals, the economic problems of developing countries, the motivations of consumers, the effects of minimum wage laws, deregulation of industries, resistance to change, and a host of other issues are explained far more accurately by evolutionary economics than by mainstream models.

Dissent from the mainstream can tell us much about how consumers actually do behave, how some economic laws fail to describe reality, and how the evolutionary principles of Charles Darwin may be more useful in describing the economy than the natural law-based scientific mechanics of Isaac Newton. This dissent can also show how such dynamic concepts as circular and cumulative causation[6] as well as path dependency[7] can be more insightful than the static equilibrium concept upon which mainstream analysis is based.

Veblen and his followers are especially critical of the concept of equilibrium because it implies something normal, natural, or even good. Equilibrium is also a static concept that defines a position of rest. The overall economy and even its individual markets, however, are constantly changing and never tend toward anything approaching such a restful spot.

Equilibrium is a contrived, artificial concept. To achieve an equilibrium price, for example, all but a single determinant of either demand or supply must be held constant. In reality, however, technology, consumer incomes, and several institutions are constantly changing. These changes are important, are worthy of careful consideration, and are far more interesting than whether or not something as unrealistic and imaginary as equilibrium is attained.

Equilibrium is disturbed by an outside event A that changes B, producing a new stable equilibrium. The change is one directional, there are no feedbacks from B to A, and the story basically ends until some new outside disturbance is introduced. As a result, the analysis is fairly static and only partially accurate. Under *circular and cumulative causation*, A changes B, which then affects A, further impacting B, and so on. Other events (C, D, E, etc.) may also be affected by the initial disturbance. There is no equilibrium or stable resting place. In addition, the concept of equilibrium suggested or implied a benevolent or at least natural outcome, whereas under circular and cumulative causation, the continuous cycle may be proceeding either toward beneficial or harmful results.

This concept will be explained more fully in the following chapter.

Broadly defined, *path dependency* means that history matters. What has occurred before, perhaps by design but more likely by chance, has set in motion a sequence of events that has followed a given direction or path. More narrowly defined, feedback provided to the existing path is often self-reinforcing, which means that the established path proceeds without modification. This view emphasizes the self-reinforcing nature of institutions. A chance experiment, for example, may lead to the development of a given technology that prompts additional uses of that technology without adequately surveying viable alternatives.

For many years, all movies were made in Hollywood, all cars were made in Michigan, most books were published in New York, and most computer chips were made in California's Silicon Valley. There may have been advantageous reasons for locating at each sight originally but businesses remained there long after those initial advantages had vanished.

For almost a century, steel manufacturing in the United States was based on the Bessemer and open hearth processes developed in the 1890s. Even after Japanese and European manufacturers adopted more modern techniques after World War II, American producers stuck with the old way until nearly the 21st century. In many government bureaucracies as well as in corporate offices, things continue to be done much the same as they have for many years.

Until very recently, all cars were powered by gasoline. Once the technology was established, a general reluctance to change dictated that the change did not occur. Much like circular and cumulative causation, the accepted path may be moving toward either a beneficial or harmful outcome. In both cases, there is no equilibrium in sight.

Institutional dissent can provide measures of

efficiency based on: 1) making the best use of human potential instead of simply minimizing costs, 2) evidence of increasing returns (especially to human knowledge) instead of blind acceptance of supposedly inevitable diminishing returns, 3) experimentation to see what actually works, and 4) a theory of government that is more meaningful than the simple desire to limit and criticize it.

In the formulation of economic policy, institutional dissent: 1) explicitly addresses the role of *power* and how those who have it can use it to their advantage, 2) more accurately shows how resistance to change in poor countries inhibits economic progress there, and 3) logically documents how corporate corruption is more of an established pattern than an occasional exception to generally upstanding behavior.

Institutional emphasis on case studies in industry, actual rather than theoretical results of deregulation and minimum wage laws, and subtle forms of industrial sabotage provide a practical framework for viewing issues involving real, not hypothetical or "representative", business firms. To fully appreciate the mainstream–evolutionary controversy, how both positions have evolved over time must be surveyed and critically analyzed.

Continued emphasis within the profession on some of the more obviously dated and questionable concepts in areas like consumer behavior and pure competition has made the discipline subject to ridicule by those in other fields, and an easy target at that. This is probably most evident in the social sciences, humanities, and business. Beginning students in such subjects as psychology, philosophy, history, and marketing all learn concepts and are exposed to examples that contradict what is taught in mainstream microeconomics. In marketing, for example, most textbooks on the theory of consumer behavior do not even mention what mainstream economists have said about the subject.

The mainstream of the discipline has achieved rather limited empirical verification of its theories. Instead, it has turned inward and imposed more rigor, including advanced mathematics, on models which has made them more analytically impressive even if not more widely applicable. The result has been the emergence of a "law" of diminishing relevance and, not at all surprisingly, waning interest which at times is even manifested in fewer students taking economics courses.

To many evolutionary economists, mainstream model building is little more than mental masturbation. It feels good while you are doing it but afterward you realize that little of any value has been accomplished and contributions to human progress have been negligible.

Major Participants in the Controversy

Mainstream economics may be interpreted as based on *selected* writings of Adam Smith and his classical disciples, including David Ricardo, Thomas Malthus, J. B. Say, Jeremy Bentham, John Stuart Mill, and others. Several decades later, *some* of their ideas were supported, refined, and made more precise by such neoclassical writers as Leon Walras, William Stanley Jevons, Carl Menger, Hermann Gossen, John Bates Clark, and especially Alfred Marshall.[8] Together, their nineteenth-century thinking fit nicely with the views of then notable non-economists.

This group included *Social Darwinists* Herbert Spencer and William Graham Sumner, some prominent literary figures including Jane Austen and Robert Browning, more mediocre writers such as Horatio Alger, and prosperous business tycoons such as John D. Rockefeller, Cornelius Vanderbilt, Jay Gould, and J. P. Morgan. The overall success of the American economy in the late nineteenth century offered general support for these optimistic observations, as well as hope that those who had not yet attained the American Dream would one day get there, if they persevered.

The criticism of Karl Marx, in some areas more perceptive than others, has been rather flippantly dismissed by mainstream observers as naïve, politically extreme, and generally discredited by world events. The dissent of Thorstein Veblen, by contrast, has in a number of cases proven to be more insightful and more accurate than more analytically precise mainstream concepts. And yet, the work of Veblen and his numerous followers has been largely ignored by, and considered irrelevant to, mainstream thinking.

Evolutionary economics may be viewed as based on the writings of Veblen, John R. Commons, Wesley C. Mitchell, Clarence E. Ayres, Gunnar Myrdal, John Kenneth Galbraith, and others. Although diverse and not always in agreement with each other, their approaches are a dissent against the mainstream tradition as exemplified by narrowly selected interpretations of Smith and Marshall. The rise of corporate giants near the end of the nineteenth century provided a model of business that was different from those offered by the mainstream. The observed behavior of consumers then and now provided patterns that were not accurately explained by the mainstream. In these areas and in others, evolutionary positions have directly challenged established doctrines within the discipline.

Some professional economists may object to the division of its members into two camps, *mainstream (neoclassical)* vs. *evolutionary (institutionalist)* as imprecise or even misleading. Those in the mainstream might point to several differences between their contemporary views and those of the neoclassicals. The modern version, however, is deeply rooted in the thought of nineteenth-century neoclassical economists, many of whose ideas are accepted by mainstreamers today.

Similarly, there are different groups who now call

themselves evolutionary economists, including some who do not trace their origins to Veblen. Most contemporary followers of Veblen call themselves institutionalists even though Veblen would have preferred the term evolutionary economics. Two recently formed groups, one called the *new institutional economics* and the other *contemporary evolutionary economics,* have little or nothing to do with either Veblen or the original "old" institutionalists. Such squabbling over names aside, the distinction made here appears justified based on the arguments made in the following pages, the historical origin of these terms, and the intellectual influences on both traditions.

Conclusion

The mainstream approach suggests that certain economic concepts "always were" and by implication "always will be". All that is needed is that these concepts be made more analytically rigorous. The evolutionary approach argues that rigor, where appropriate, is exceedingly useful but that history has shown the inevitability of change that is sometimes quite dramatic. For an economics discipline to be relevant, it must develop methods capable of analyzing that change.

Footnotes:

1. Paul A. Samuelson, "What Classical and Neoclassical Monetary Theory Really Was", *Canadian Journal of Economics*, 1, 1, (February 1968), pp. 1-15.

2. Reading Veblen in the original is not an easy task. For the best summary of his ideas in readable form, see Ken McCormick, *Veblen in Plain English: A Complete Introduction to Thorstein Veblen's Economics,* (Youngstown,

New York: Cambria Press, 2006).

3. David Dequech, "The Institutions of Economics: A First Approximation", *Journal of Economic Issues,* 48, 2 (June 2014), pp. 523-531.

4. This dichotomy has been modified by several researchers since first formally presented by Ayres in 1962 (*The Theory of Economic Progress*, 2nd ed., New York: Schocken Books) and utilized more extensively by Wendell Gordon in 1980 (*Institutional Economics: The Changing System,* Austin, University of Texas Press). Most of this work involved various "updates" so that more recent issues could be analyzed within this framework. One study (Igor Matutinovic, "An Institutional Approach to Sustainability: Historical Interplay of Worldviews, Institutions, and Technology", *Journal of Economic Issues*, 41, 4 (December 2007), pp. 1109-1137), for example, has broadened the approach to include the concept of "worldview" and its potential impact on sustainability. Such updates, while valuable for some current research, are less relevant in studying the issues considered here.

5. Joseph E. Pluta, "Evolutionary Economics and Microeconomic Principles" in Krishna Kishore Puranam and Ravi Kumar Jain B, (eds.) *Evolutionary Economics*, (Hyderabad, India: Icfai University Press, 2008).

6. For a recent summary of the literature on this topic, see Joseph E. Pluta, "Evolutionary Alternatives to Equilibrium Economics: Some Suggested Applications", *American Journal of Economics and Sociology,* 69, 4 (October 2010), pp. 1155-1177. See also Sebastian Berger, ed. *The Foundations of Non-Equilibrium Economics: The Principle of Circular and Cumulative Causation*, (London: Routledge,

2009).

7. William Barnes, Myles Gartland, and Martin Stack, "Old Habits Die Hard: Path Dependency and Behavioral Lock-in," *Journal of Economic Issues,* 38, 2 (June 2004), pp. 371–377.

As the following sources indicate, the concept is widely used in several disciplines besides economics. See Raghu Garud, Arun Kumaraswamy, and Peter Karnoe, "Path Dependence or Path Creation?" *Journal of Management Studies*, 47, 2 (June 2010), pp. 760-774; Taylor C. Boas, "Conceptualizing Continuity and Change: The Composite-Standard Model of Path Dependence", *Journal of Theoretical Politics*, 19, 1 (January 2007), pp. 33-54; and James Mahoney, "Path Dependence in Historical Sociology", *Theory and Society*, 29, 4 (August 2000), pp. 507-548.

8. For a concise yet thorough background on many of these economists, see E. Ray Canterbury, *A Brief History of Economics: Artful Approaches to the Dismal Science,* 2nd ed., (Singapore: World Scientific Publishing Company, 2010).

Chapter Three

Building a Discipline on a Metaphor

The reason that the invisible hand often seems invisible is that it is often not there.
Joseph Stiglitz

Capitalism is the astounding belief that the most wickedest of men will do the most wickedest of things for the greatest good of everyone.
John Maynard Keynes

Equilibrium is a figment of the human imagination.
Kenneth E. Boulding

In his 1776 classic *The Wealth of Nations,* Adam Smith emphasized, among other things, that competition enabled the economy to regulate itself. To build his argument, he presented the metaphor of the invisible hand, his observation that the pursuit of self-interest automatically guarantees that the public good is served. This countered the mercantilist view that strong central government direction was essential. To Smith, the (highly visible hand of) government could be replaced by the (invisible hand of the) market with better results.

Writing during the age of corporate excess at the turn of the previous century, Thorstein Veblen challenged this concept by arguing that it had only been asserted, never tested, and certainly not proven. According to Veblen, the robber barons of his day pursued their own self-interest and guaranteed only that their interests were served at the expense of the public good. In recent years, economists including John Kenneth Galbraith and others[1] have echoed Veblen's critique and have witnessed much dubious corporate behavior to support their case.

Despite these challenges, the invisible hand metaphor is still faithfully recited as if it were a central proposition in divine revelation. In mainstream economics, producers are assumed to pursue their self-interest by maximizing profit while consumers are assumed to pursue their self-interest by maximizing utility in their purchases. Moreover, competitive equilibrium, the cornerstone of Alfred Marshall's nineteenth century market model, continues to elicit support among mainstream economists and many historians of economic thought.[2] The general success of free markets compared with alternative economic systems over time has reassured many observers that Smith was at least on the right track and that competition is a fairly effective regulatory device.

The precision of the mainstream market model is analytically impressive. There are, however, several larger questions at issue in this analysis. Does it give a complete and accurate picture of what it is attempting to describe? In the interest of rigor and quantification, is anything being sacrificed? What else should be central to the description and analysis? If the concept of equilibrium is deficient, what method of inquiry may be used in its place? In their critique of the neoclassical approach, evolutionary economists address several mainstream shortcomings and propose alternative ways of understanding the economy.

Some Trouble Spots

Although the market model is valuable for what it does, it is also limited by what it does not do and cannot do. Veblen saw equilibrium as implying something positive, which might not be so. Just because a market tends toward a given price and quantity does not mean that such a result is necessarily beneficial to all concerned. High prices for gasoline, for example, might be nice for oil companies and their stockholders but are devastating to consumers, especially those with limited incomes, and to all businesses that use petroleum products as a resource. In addition, Veblen's followers today suggest that in many markets, including those for gasoline, multiple prices are just as likely as any single price.[3] In these cases, they ask, of what value is an alleged single equilibrium price, no matter how elegant the mechanism that produces this result? In fact, the mechanism may be seriously flawed if it predicts a single price when multiple prices exist.

More troubling is the fact that, in order to reach an equilibrium, several factors on both the demand side (tastes, income, expectations, etc.) and the supply side (technology, resource prices, number of firms, etc.) must be held constant. The important point raised by Veblen and his followers is that *all of these factors are, in fact, constantly changing, and those changes are not only important but require explanation.*[4] Further, the dynamics involved in all of these factors are frankly more interesting than whether or not something artificial called equilibrium is reached. For example, the story of how new technology has been developed and its profound impact on lifestyles, according to this critique, should be at center stage in the study of economics and not merely a factor assumed to be unchanged. Assuming away the most fascinating aspects of the process is neither scientific nor particularly enlightening.

The market model also assumes that demand and supply are completely independent of each other. In other words, none of the factors that determine demand also determine supply. This independence helps the model work smoothly and with minimal complication. Veblen has shown instances, however, where *this disconnect simply is not true.*[5] If consumer incomes rise, for example, demand for normal goods will clearly increase. But the surge in income will also likely stimulate business investment in new technology that will cause supply to rise as well. Similarly, an increase in supply without higher incomes would not guarantee that the added output would be purchased. This could result in general overproduction and an economic downturn. The market model, however, would merely predict that lower prices would cause quantity demanded to rise to the level of the new quantity supplied. A danger, therefore, exists in studying small parts of the economy separated from the whole. A broad perspective, including input from disciplines other than economics, enables a better understanding of how various parts of the economy interrelate.

Veblen's disciples today also question the assumptions that "the market way of doing things" is permanent, is inevitably spreading to all parts of the world, and is somehow part of a universally benevolent system.[6] Such a naive scenario ignores the wealth and power possessed by corporations, banks, and a handful of individuals. The market model, in other words, may perform adequately in a world of many small producers, none of whom has a competitive edge. Unfortunately, however, the power of giant corporations that produce goods and the huge banks that finance their activities, *both legal and illegal,* is downplayed if not ignored in the mainstream market model. These are the same mammoth entities who attempt to manipulate government policy in their favor by making sizable contributions to political candidates who support their interests. Galbraith has offered some of the most cogent observations of well-orchestrated corporate deception in this area.[7]

Spokespersons for these economically elite mega-firms may publicly embrace the rhetoric of minimal government and may shamelessly praise the benefits of competition, but they are quite clever and effective in getting government support to limit competition. Tariffs on foreign goods are a prime example. The power of a small group of producers or the wealth of a small number of consumers may clearly influence market outcomes in ways the market model can only partially explain. The market model, therefore, either ignores the distribution of income or downplays its effects even though how income and wealth are distributed plays a key role in determining price and output.

Among the many actors in the economic game, there are several different groups with different and often conflicting economic interests. Corporations, small businesses, unions, consumers, farmers, urban residents, employers, workers, bankers, insurance companies, and others clearly pursue different goals and may be affected differently by price changes or by government policies. Smith's invisible hand metaphor and the type of analysis his followers developed suggest a "harmony of interests" approach: a similarity in goals and in the benefits that the market system makes possible. Given the obvious differences in the interests of, say, workers and employers, a "conflict of interests" approach appears more appropriate. As a result, the market model is often criticized for its overly optimistic view of the way things work when conflict rather than harmony may be the more normal situation.

Veblen Goods

A more fundamental and potentially disturbing question concerns the slope of the demand curve and one of Marshall's famous laws. Specifically, is the law of demand ever violated? Veblen challenged this law, arguing that, when people are motivated by conspicuous consumption, they will buy *more,* not less, of a good at a higher price. When goods are consumed in order to impress others, one must demonstrate that the masses cannot afford them. Only in this way is status achieved. Especially conspicuous is expenditure that is wasteful. Enormous homes; numerous servants; automobiles that ordinary people could not possibly afford; imported luxuries including expensive works of art, rare pets, exotic foreign vacations; and designer clothes all are signs of either membership in the leisure class or a desire to emulate their lifestyles. Veblen used the term *pecuniary emulation* to describe the desire of consumers to imitate the spending habits of those who are above them in social status. To evolutionary economists, therefore, conspicuous consumption and pecuniary emulation should be considered determinants of demand.

Given status seeking behavior, if the price is low, there is little reason to buy goods which are accessible to the mass market. Goods in which price and quantity demanded are directly related have come to be known as *Veblen goods* and can easily be illustrated with an upward sloping demand curve[8] or some variation[9] thereof. When exclusivity is the goal, the standard downward-sloping demand curve may not be relevant. An upward-sloping demand curve may be an important expression of Veblen's larger rejection of mainstream logic.

An Alternative to Equilibrium

In contrast to Adam Smith's market-regulated economy, the critique of Veblen and others argues that the economy is regulated by several institutions, of which the market is only one.[10] Since institutions are habits of thought (like custom and tradition), established social practices (like human behavior and family life), and forms of organization (like markets, business firms large and small, banks, governments, and a legal system), all of these things together regulate the economy and influence prices. In this view, the ever-changing cumulative effects of adaptation, crisis, trial and error, instability, and movement tell us more about how an economy performs, how it is regulated, and how its prices are set than equilibrium does. In other words, economic life is regulated more by institutions that vary by place and over time than by economic laws such as the laws of supply and demand, which are static and are often erroneously considered to be timeless.

In place of equilibrium, many evolutionary economists propose an alternative concept called *circular and cumulative causation.*[11] Originally advanced by Veblen, the idea was developed more fully by Swedish Nobel Laureate Gunnar Myrdal (1898–1987).[12] Equilibrium is disturbed by an outside event A that changes B, producing a new stable equilibrium. The change is one-directional, there are no feedbacks from B to A, and the story basically ends until some new outside disturbance is introduced. As a result, the analysis is fairly static and only partially accurate. Under circular and cumulative causation, A changes B, which then affects A, further impacting B, and so on. Other events (C, D, E, etc.) may also be affected by the initial disturbance. There is no equilibrium or stable resting place. In addition, the concept of equilibrium suggested or implied a benevolent or at least natural outcome. Under circular and cumulative causation, the continuous cycle may be proceeding either toward beneficial or harmful results.

Two contemporary examples, one with largely positive and the other with highly negative outcomes, illustrate how this concept works. On the positive side, suppose technological advance occurs. Mainstream supply and demand analysis would suggest that improved technology (event A) shifts the supply curve to the right, resulting in higher output and lower prices (event B). A new equilibrium is reached and is maintained until a new, and completely independent, disturbance inaugurates its own response.

Under circular and cumulative causation, however, multiple events result from the initial advance in technology (event A). Clearly, the output of firms in a given region that uses this technology increases (event B). But this added output also means the region has become more productive (event C), which makes that region more competitive (event D) compared to its neighbors with which it trades. Greater competitiveness causes prices in the region to fall (event E), which will cause its exports to increase (event F). Perhaps most importantly, greater exports cause output to rise again (event B), which causes the entire sequence to repeat itself. Figure 1 shows the generally beneficial outcome of this whole process far more completely than neoclassical supply and demand curves.[13]

Figure 1

Circular and Cumulative Causation
With Generally Beneficial Outcome

Event A (Technological Advance) ➔

Event B (Output Increases) ➔

Event C (Productivity Increases) ➔

Event D (Competitiveness Increases) ➔

Event E (Price Level Falls) ➔

Event F (Exports Increase) ➔

Event B (Output Increases) ➔ ……

Unfavorable results may occur in the following manner. Suppose a local manufacturing firm in the Midwest shuts down and moves its operations to Mexico where labor is less expensive. Mainstream supply and demand analysis tells us that, in this Midwestern community or region, the exit of firms from the industry (event A) causes supply to shift to the left, resulting in less output and higher prices (event B). A new equilibrium is supposedly reached and the market remains in this position until some new event is forthcoming.

The circular and cumulative causation framework presents a somewhat different picture. Firm exit (event A) certainly causes output in the region to fall and the reduced availability of goods makes prices higher (event B). Event B, however, may further impact event A, as lower output in a now economically depressed region may cause other firms to exit from the region. This process may result in a rather substantial downward economic spiral. Event A and B together will clearly cause unemployment to rise (event C), and many unemployed workers may lose their homes (event D). This may cause workers to seek jobs in other local businesses or to migrate from the area entirely (event E). The community itself will become economically depressed (event F), which will cause exit of yet more firms (event A) and a repeat of the cycle.

Figure 2 shows the generally negative outcome of this whole process far more completely than neoclassical supply and demand curves.[14] Further, even more negative effects may be introduced as such noneconomic factors as increased psychological depression (event G), rising crime rates (event H), family discord (event I) and other events (J, K, L, etc.) result.

Figure 2

Circular and Cumulative Causation
With Generally Harmful Outcome

Event A (Firms Exit) ➔

Event B (Output Falls, Prices Rise) ➔
Event A (More Fims Exit) ➔
Event B (Output Falls, Prices Rise) ➔
Event C (Unemployment Rises) ➔

Event D (Workers Lose Homes) ➔

Event E (Workers Leave Area) ➔

Event F (Area Becomes Economically Depressed)➔
Event A (More Firms Exit) ➔
Event B (Again Output Falls, Prices Rise) ➔
Event C (Unemployment Rises Further) ➔
Event D (More Workers Lose Homes) ➔
Event G (Psychological Disorders) ➔

Event H (Rising Crime Rates) ➔

Event I (Family Discord) ➔
Event E (More Workers Leave Area) ➔
Event F (More Economic Depression) ➔
Event A (More Firms Exit) ➔ ....

Events J, K, L (Other Non-Economic Problems)
➔ Event H (Rising Crime Rates) ➔......

Sample Applications

Myrdal was commissioned by the Carnegie Commission in the United States to study American race relations on the eve of World War II. Many of the results of his study were based on the cumulative causation principle.[15] Among his arguments, which drew on noneconomic as well as economic factors, the following three were illustrative.

First, prejudice against African Americans produced lower standards of living for them. Observing these lower living standards, white Americans felt their prejudice was justified. This generated additional declines in African American living standards relative to whites.

Secondly, poor educational opportunities for African Americans made it less likely that they would either enter the medical profession or be knowledgeable about health and sanitation. Their lower incomes often denied African Americans access to high quality health care. As a result, they were more likely than whites to be in poor health which made it more difficult to secure jobs that paid well. With lower incomes, African American education is likely to remain inferior and the cycle repeats itself.

Thirdly, what can be done to reverse the downward cumulative process and turn it upward? American institutions such as churches, schools, trade unions, and government were designated by Myrdal to lead the charge in reducing prejudice, increasing educational opportunities for minorities, guaranteeing the right to vote without intimidation, and encouraging migration out of the then more racist South into regions which were more racially tolerant and where better paying jobs existed.

This institutional change ultimately was a major factor in enhancing economic opportunities for African Americans and other minorities. The market adapted to these changing circumstances but was not in itself an agent for change. *It is hard to imagine what the concept of equilibrium had to do with any of these monumental and progressive changes in American culture.*

Much economic analysis today uses Myrdal's pioneering model with penetrating insightful analyses and favorable results. Cumulative causation has been used to explain complex relationships in American industry, persistent poverty in depressed U.S. neighborhoods and in underdeveloped countries, the successful manufacturing strategies pursuing economic growth in post–World War II Japan, and appropriate policies for encouraging growth in regions that seek it. The holistic approach that broadly views dynamic change holds enormous potential as a multidisciplinary tool of analysis. In Myrdal's own words:

> The dynamics of this social system are determined by the fact that . . . there is circular causation, implying that, if there is change in one condition, others will change in response. Those secondary changes in their turn will cause new changes all around, even affecting the condition whose change we assumed initiated the process, and so on in further rounds. So the whole system will be moving in one direction or another, and it may even be turning around. . . . There is no one basic factor; everything causes everything else. This implies interdependence within the whole social process. And there is generally no equilibrium in sight.[16]

Evolutionary economists see other problems with the idea of a unique price being determined by the laws of supply and demand. Over the years, several studies have documented fairly long periods when prices did not change despite the fact that several determinants of demand and supply did. One of the more popular arguments has been the *theory of administered prices*, originally advanced by Gardiner Means during the 1930s.[17] Among other things, this theory argues that, despite a fall in demand that would normally produce lower prices, large firms with market power can conspire to prevent prices from falling. When actual managers have been interviewed, prices have been shown to be set by a strategy that estimates the firm's costs and then adds in a mark-up according to a variety of possible methods. A number of research efforts by institutional economists are currently under way to use cumulative causation, administered pricing, the role of economic power, mark-up strategies, and other non–mainstream concepts to develop a better explanation of how prices are determined than the supply and demand model.[18]

The Minimum Wage Issue

Evolutionary economists have recently added an additional element to one of the most controversial issues in all of economics. For many years, the orthodox neoclassical position, based on the use of the market model (supply and demand curves), has claimed that minimum wage laws *cause* unemployment. Recent research, however, challenges this view.[19] Studies of the fast-food industry in New Jersey and Pennsylvania have found that, not only did a higher minimum wage *not* cause unemployment, but *higher minimum wages actually caused the number of jobs in the industry to increase.* Although higher minimum wages did lead to higher prices for meals, prices did not rise any more in those restaurants that had the largest number of employees working for the minimum wage. In addition, no restaurants were forced to close because they had to pay higher wages.[20]

How can these results be explained when the market model predicts the opposite will occur? The fast-food industry is the dominant employer of relatively unskilled workers in most regions of the country. This means that these workers have few or no options for alternative employment. They either work for the low wages paid by restaurants or they do not work at all. The increase in wages paid draws more people into the labor force and creates a greater incentive for them to work. Healthier and more eager workers are more productive, less likely to quit, and more attractive to employers who therefore are more willing to hire them. It has further been documented that higher minimum wages have caused employers in the fast-food industry to hire more teenage workers, not fewer as popular opinion alleges.[21]

Sometimes, the number of jobs *rises* after minimum wage increases because employers engage in rescheduling. Required to pay higher wages, employers do experience an increase in labor costs *per hour.* They therefore hire more workers for fewer hours. While this may seem like a mixed blessing for workers, hours in New Jersey restaurants fell only by 6 percent, roughly an hour and fifteen minutes per week.[22] Two additional studies across several different industries found that not only had small businesses not been negatively affected by the 1997 minimum wage increase but also that most would not have been harmed had that minimum wage increase been higher (up to $7.25 per hour).[23]

The evolutionary view has long been that economic theories have value only when they are submitted to testing and are verified as facts. In this case, the market model and popular folklore say one thing while facts say another.

Some institutional economists have recently argued that minimum wages (1) stimulate demand for products, (2) encourage firms to develop and use the latest technology, and (3) equalize bargaining power in labor markets.[24] On the first point, low-income individuals spend a higher percentage of their incomes than others do. The working poor also tend to spend their money on domestically produced goods such as food, rent, and goods sold by local small businesses rather than on overseas vacations or stock market speculation. Spending on the former provides more jobs within the United States while spending on overseas vacations clearly does not. Minimum wages, therefore, promote growth in the domestic economy.

On the second point, firms faced with higher wages have an incentive to develop or use existing labor-saving technology, which makes those firms more productive. Especially in restaurants, such options are relatively few. Most, including kitchen equipment and webpages, may have already been realized. Such technology has done more to make firms efficient than to eliminate jobs. On the third point, the minimum wage enables low-income individuals to earn a living, achieve some level of human dignity, and enjoy bargaining power similar to that possessed by members of labor unions.

In 2014, proposals to raise the minimum wage to $10.10 per hour were stalled by a reluctant Congress. Its opposition was fueled by the usual litany of arguments. This time, the negative employment effects were alleged to occur because jobs would be outsourced while the federal deficit would rise to fund wage increases. It is difficult to imagine how fast food restaurants could possibly outsource the flipping of hamburgers to workers in China, Mexico, or the Philippines and serve this food to customers here in the U. S. In addition, several of these businesses currently pay wages so low that many of its employees qualify for public assistance. When removed from these rolls, might burdens on taxpayers be lessened by a slight increase in the price of the Big Mac?

Those who decry the "severe" inflation such price increases will cause would do well to compare the bill for minimum wage increases with the ten billion dollar per month price tag to finance the Bush-Cheney-Rumsfeld venture in Iraq. Launched to give Cheney's Halliburton energy firm first shot at Iraqi oil, the result put billions of profit into the pockets of Halliburton executives. The effect on the federal deficit was enormous. Even ignoring the thousands of deaths to American military personnel and Iraqi women and children plus the irreparable damage to America's image abroad this unprovoked invasion caused, the expense of a minimum wage increase would be minuscule in comparison.

Whether true or not, when something is repeated often enough, it is believed by some people. This appears to be the case with the argument that minimum wage laws cause unemployment. That such an argument is cloaked in an inaccurate mainstream principle is difficult to justify.

Research done by institutional economists and others concludes the following: *Minimum wages benefit, rather than harm, those low income workers who receive them. Very few, if any, of these workers lose their jobs because of minimum wage laws. Some evidence even exists that minimum wage legislation helps to create additional jobs.* These are the observed facts and they are *inconsistent* with mainstream economic theory.[25]

One final observation can be made. Two similar retail chains, Walmart and Costco, directly compete in numerous markets. Walmart is notorious for its low wages, high employee turnover, and number of employees who qualify for public assistance. Costco pays substantially higher wages and avoids time spent in retraining workers because turnover is minimal. More importantly, Costco in recent years has been substantially *more profitable* than Walmart.

Is it possible that employees who are paid well are more dedicated, more loyal, and more productive than workers who are paid poorly and treated with indifference? Does the mainstream argument that paying higher wages makes a firm less competitive have any validity here whatsoever? And finally, if workers are poorly paid (and more and more jobs are outsourced to other countries), who is going to buy the goods American firms are producing?

Mainstream arguments that higher wages make American businesses less competitive might want to consider a larger issue. If American workers are paid on a scale anywhere near what workers in poor countries are paid, do we want the widespread poverty here that exists in those countries?

Conclusion

Although the existence of equilibrium in markets, and certainly the tendency toward a *single* price, has been rather difficult to prove, mainstream analysis somehow remains the tool of preference in the profession. Although models that employ the equilibrium approach undoubtedly abstract from reality, to many people their analyses appear sound. Focus on a limited number of variables, this argument alleges, is more workable than including a more thorough abundance of factors, some of which are difficult to quantify.

Evolutionary economists, however, continue to emphasize the importance of a multidisciplinary, broad-based approach to analyzing the economy. They also argue that including multiple descriptive factors may be more complicated, possibly less neat and concise, but clearly more dynamic and realistic than the picture presented by the mainstream neoclassical approach. The roles played by institutions and by human imperfection (behavior that is multifaceted and unpredictable in the cases of both consumers and producers) clearly matter in an analysis and an understanding of the economy. The market is merely one of those institutions.

Footnotes:

1. Mathew T. Clements, "Self-Interest vs. Greed and the Limitations of the Invisible Hand", *American Journal of*

Economics and Sociology, 72, 4 (October 2013), pp. 949-965.

2. Roger E. Backhouse, "History and Equilibrium: A Partial Defense of Equilibrium Economics," *Journal of Economic Methodology,* 11, 3 (September 2004), pp. 291–305.

3. Fred S. McChesney, William F. Shughart II, and David D. Haddock, "On the Internal Contradictions of the Law of One Price," *Economic Inquiry,* 42, 3 (October 2004), pp. 706–716, and Daniel R. Fusfeld, "A Manifesto for Institutional Economics," *Journal of Economic Issues,* 34, 2 (June 2000), p. 259.

4. Wendell Gordon, *Institutional Economics: The Changing System,* (Austin: University of Texas Press, 1980), pp. 97–111.

5. Philip A. O'Hara, "The Contemporary Relevance of Thorstein Veblen's Institutional-Evolutionary Political Economy," *History of Economics Review,* 35, 1 (Winter 2002), p. 89.

6. Francis Fukuyama, *The End of History and the Last Man,* (New York: Avon Books, 1992).

7. Stephen P. Dunn and Steven Pressman, "The Economic Contributions of John Kenneth Galbraith," *Review of Political Economy,* 17, 2 (April 2005), pp. 161–209 and John Kenneth Galbraith, *The Essential Galbraith,* (Boston: Houghton Mifflin, 2001).

8. Harvey Leibenstein, "Bandwagon, Snob, and Veblen Effects in the Theory of Consumer's Demand," *Quarterly Journal of Economics,* 64, 2 (May 1950), pp. 183–207.

9. Zvavka Todorova, "Conspicuous Consumption as Routine Expenditure and its Place in the Social Provisioning Process", *American Journal of Economics and Sociology*, 72, 5 (November 2013), pp. 1183-1204 and E. Ray Canterbery, "The Theory of the Leisure Class and the Theory of Demand," in Warren J. Samuels, ed., *The Founding of Institutional Economics: The Leisure Class and Sovereignty,* (New York: Routledge, 1998), pp. 140–141.

10. Theofanis Papageorgiou, Ioannis Katselidis, and Panayotis G. Michaelides, "Schumpeter, Commons, and Veblen on Institutions", *American Journal of Economics and Sociology*, 72, 5 (November 2013), pp. 1232-1254 and Eduaro Fernandez-Huerga, "The Market Concept: A Characterization from Institutional and Post-Keynesian Economics", *American Journal of Economics and Sociology*, 72, 2 (April 2013), pp. 361-385.

11. Some of the discussion of CCC draws on an earlier work of mine. See Joseph E. Pluta, "Evolutionary Alternatives to Equilibrium Economics: Some Suggested Applications", *American Journal of Economics and Sociology*, 69, 4 (October 2010): pp. 1155-1177.

12. Others credited with either initiating or promoting a version of this concept include Knut Wicksell, Allyn Young, and Nicholas Kaldor. A good summary of the major arguments may be found in Phillip Toner, *Main Currents in Cumulative Causation: The Dynamics of Growth and Development,* (London: Macmillan, 1999).

13. This figure is adapted from a similar illustration in Harvey W. Armstrong and Jim Taylor, *Regional Economics and Policy,* 3rd ed., (London: Blackwell Publishing, 2000), p. 97, Figure 4.2.

14. This figure is based on the story in Michael Moore's documentary film *Roger and Me.* The film is about the closing of General Motors plants in Flint, Michigan and the subsequent effects on the community that can be analyzed using the circular and cumulative causation framework. A course at Mount Holyoke College maintains a Web site titled *Economics in Film* where a number of posts by students addressed the use of Myrdal's concept in this documentary.

15. Gunnar Myrdal, *An American Dilemma,* (New York: Harper and Brothers, 1944), especially pp. 381, 172, and 198. These arguments are nicely summarized in Steven Pressman, *Fifty Major Economists,* 2nd ed., (London: Routledge, 2006), pp. 171–172.

16. Gunnar Myrdal, "Institutional Economics," *Journal of Economic Issues,* 12, 4 (December 1978), pp. 771–785.

17. Gardiner C. Means, "The Administered Price Theory Reconfirmed," *American Economic Review,* 62, 3 (September 1972), pp. 292–306.

18. Mark Nichols, Oleg Pavlov, and Michael J. Radzicki, "The Circular and Cumulative Structure of Administered Pricing," *Journal of Economic Issues,* 40, 2 (June 2006), pp. 517–526.

19. Some of this research is nicely summarized in Oren M. Levin-Waldman, "Why the Minimum Wage Orthodoxy Reigns Supreme", *Challenge, 58*, 1 (January/February 2015), pp. 29-50. For an earlier study, see Oren M. Levin-Waldman, "Policy Orthodoxies, the Minimum Wage, and the Challenge of Social Science," *Journal of Economic Issues,* 38, 1 (March 2004), pp. 139–154.

20. David Card and Alan B. Krueger, "A Reanalysis of the Effect of the New Jersey Minimum Wage Increase on the Fast-Food Industry with Representative Payroll Data," Working Paper no. 6386, National Bureau of Economic Research, 1998; David Card and Alan B. Krueger, *Myth and Measurement: The New Economics of the Minimum Wage,* (Princeton, NJ: Princeton University Press, 1995); and Lawrence F. Katz and Alan B. Krueger, "The Effect of the Minimum Wage on the Fast-Food Industry," *Industrial and Labor Relations Review,* 46, 1 (October 1992), pp. 6–21.

21. Kevin Lang and Shulamit Kahn, "The Effect of Minimum-Wage Laws on the Distribution of Employment: Theory and Evidence," *Journal of Public Economics,* 69, 1 (July 1998), pp. 67–82.

22. Thomas R. Michl, "Can Rescheduling Explain the New Jersey Minimum Wage Studies?" *Eastern Economic Journal,* 26, 3 (Summer 2000), pp. 265–276.

23. Oren M. Levin-Waldman, "The Minimum Wage Can Be Raised: Lessons from the 1999 Levy Survey of Small Business," *Challenge,* 43, 2 (March/April 2000), pp. 86–96 and Oren M. Levin-Waldman, "The Effects of the Minimum Wage: A Business Response," *Journal of Economic Issues,* 34, 3 (September 2000), pp. 723–730.

24. Robert E. Prasch, "In Defense of the Minimum Wage," *Journal of Economic Issues,* 30, 2 (June 1996), pp. 391–397.

25. For an *extensive* up to date (2015) bibliography that refutes the mainstream claim with data on federal, state, and city minimum wage laws, see: Holly Sklar, "Research Shows Minimum Wage Increases Do Not Cause Job Loss", in *Business for a Fair Minimum Wage,* 2015. *This publication*

also contains numerous statements from small business owners nationwide that support an increase in the current minimum wage. See also Oren M. Levin-Waldman, "The Broad Reach of the Minimum Wage", *Challenge,* 52, 5 (September-October 2009): pp. 100-116 and Joseph E. Pluta, "Might Higher Minimum Wages Actually Create Jobs and Help Small Businesses?" *Perspectives in Business,* 6, 1 (Winter 2009), pp. 19-25.

Chapter Four

Economics and Psychology: An Evolving Relationship

Classic economic theory, based as it is on an inadequate theory of motivation, could be revolutionized by accepting the reality of higher human needs.

Abraham Maslow

Greed is a bottomless pit which exhausts the person in an endless effort to satisfy the need without ever reaching satisfaction.

Eric Fromm

Utility is a metaphysical concept of impregnable circularity; utility is the quality in commodities that makes individuals want to buy them, and the fact that individuals want to buy commodities shows that they have utility.

Joan Robinson

Civilization has been created under the pressure of the exigencies of life at the cost of satisfaction of the instincts.

Sigmund Freud

The mainstream market model is based on the notion of a *rational economic man* who is assumed to maximize utility subject to his budget constraint. Evolutionary economists believe that institutional constraints such as laws or customs may also restrict a consumer's pursuit of satisfaction. They also reject the rationality assumption and emphasize the importance of psychological factors (stress, uncertainty, fear of unemployment) in influencing choice. Adam Smith, who is often inaccurately linked to the rational consumer concept, actually proposed a theory of human nature based on a number of propensities, including emulation of the wealthy and successful. Mainstream economists, however, have ignored Smith's wider view.

A leading evolutionary economist has stated: "If rational behavior is to be assumed, then its evolution has to be explained."[1] Mainstream economists have not offered such an explanation. In addition, they have generally limited their analysis to basic economic constraints such as income and prices of goods. Their fascination with equilibrium depicts consumers as moving from one position of rest to another.

In a unique satirical writing style and with gnawing sarcastic wit, Veblen mocked this narrow neoclassical conception in a much quoted expose:

> The psychological and anthropological preconceptions of the economists have been those which were accepted by the psychological and social sciences some generations ago. The hedonistic conception of man is that of a lightning calculator of pleasure and pains, who oscillates like a homogeneous globule of desire of happiness under the impulse of stimuli that shift him about the area, but leave him intact. He has neither antecedent nor consequent. He is an isolated, definitive human datum in stable equilibrium except for the buffets of the impinging forces that displace him in one direction or another. Self-imposed in elemental space, he spins symmetrically about his own spiritual axis until the parallelogram of forces bears down

> upon him, whereupon he follows the line of the resultant. When the force of the impact is spent, he comes to rest, a self-contained globule of desire as before.[2]

Evolutionary economists today offer a range of views regarding the disposal and/or replacement of *economic man.* One writer has argued that Veblen himself viewed the concept as merely too narrow, not absolutely or even necessarily wrong.[3] Such a view suggests that the monetary drive exists but that people are also motivated by other factors. A second writer has proposed that the concept be replaced by the *socio-cultural person.*[4] Instead of single-mindedly seeking maximum satisfaction, this multidimensional individual pursues multiple goals and objectives. His or her behavior is determined by the overall environment in which this person also plays an active role. This environment is continually evolving because of the dynamic force of technological change. Yet a third writer believes that *institutionalized man* is the proper concept. His reasoning is persuasive:

> Institutionalists assume that the behavior of individuals is the product of social institutions. Prisoners quickly develop a prisoner's mentality. Presidents usually act presidential. Institutionalized man is substituted for rational man.[5]

Even allowing for some questionable presidential behavior in history, upon close examination, the three views are actually quite consistent. All challenge the mainstream position. All seek to portray human vision as wider than only economically motivated—in other words, more like people really are.

Instinct Psychology

Even when notions like rationality and utility were developed and extended during the nineteenth century, many psychologists were already questioning the philosophy of utilitarianism on which they were based. The profession (including Sigmund Freud, its leading figure) at that time embraced something called instinct psychology, which it later rejected in favor of several alternative approaches including behavioral, cognitive, evolutionary, and humanistic psychology.

Veblen was strongly influenced by instinct psychology, which viewed instincts as human motivational forces. Although he never officially defined the term *instincts,* he used them as underlying traits that guided human behavior. [6] Recall that he built his evolutionary theory around such instincts as workmanship, idle curiosity, and the parental bent. He saw these as leading to human and economic progress through the dynamic force of technology, which included human knowhow. He viewed the acquisitive instinct, however, as self-serving and potentially harmful to society through its establishment of static past-binding institutions. Human behavior based on these and other instincts, Veblen argued, was a more valid psychological foundation upon which to build a discipline of economics than rationality rooted in hedonistic utilitarianism and maximizing assumptions derived from Newtonian calculus.

Although many people might think that instincts are among the most rudimentary of human responses equivalent in the eyes of some to near animal reflexes, Veblen pointed out the difference between reactions and thoughtful motivational direction. To do this, he distinguished between tropisms and instincts. As explained by two present-day scholars,[7] *tropisms* are mere automatic physiologic responses from a received impulse while instincts involve conscious effort and intelligent adaptation toward selected ends. Tropisms, in other words, are mere reflexes. Instincts, however, "deal with complex, purposive social behavior."[8] Veblen used the terms *instincts, impulses, proclivities, propensities,* and *hereditary traits* interchangeably. He and many (but not all) of his followers believed that the motivating drive provided by instincts is a far more valid basis for analyzing human behavior than *rationality.* Veblen, however, did not adequately explain either the source of instincts or some method of determining if they even exist.[9]

Maslow's Hierarchy of Needs

Many behaviorists held a favorable view of utility theory. To the rest of the psychology profession, however, the rational economic person was considered to be an unrealistic, narrowly defined creature who was certainly rare, if he or she existed at all. *To most psychologists, therefore, belief in rational economic humans was itself irrational.* Throughout the twentieth century, various economists also became uncomfortable with specific aspects of utility theory. In an economics discipline that valued measurement, for example, utility could not be quantified and interpersonal comparisons of utility among different consumers could not easily be made. The psychology profession was quick to recognize the multidimensional aspects of human behavior that could not be reduced to strictly economic motivations.

More fundamentally, neoclassical economists and their mainstream followers based their analyses on consumer *wants,* rather than *needs.*[10] Since utility was allegedly possessed by all goods, wants were treated as essentially similar and capable of being satisfied in similar fashion by increased consumption. A college education and a new car, for example, are both human wants that can be similarly satisfied, since both add utility. Many psychologists, by contrast, would argue that the car and education satisfy different needs. Because a person experiences difficulty simultaneously pursuing multiple needs, ranking needs in some manner is not only important but essential.

By the middle of the twentieth century, noted psychologist Abraham Maslow had developed a hierarchy of needs and argued that consumers sought to satisfy basic needs first before pursuing higher ones.[11] Most basic were needs of physiology (water, food, clothing, shelter), followed by safety and security, then belongingness (acceptance, meaningful social relationships), and next, self-esteem (or a sense of self-worth). Finally, only after all these previous needs have been met, human beings strive for self-actualization (meaningfulness, aesthetics, justice, truth, love, etc.).

Lower-level needs are more materialistic while higher needs are more socially oriented and less concerned with material gain. Gratification of lower-level needs reduces their strength, but gratification of the highest needs does the reverse. If a person, for example, is able to produce something creative such as a painting, this accomplishment further stimulates desire for artistic expression and encourages an even greater pursuit of human potential. In psychology, this is a distinctly positive development that promotes fulfillment and, dare it be said, happiness.

In pursuit of higher-level needs, therefore, more goods are not better than less goods. A basic assumption of mainstream economics has been violated. If this perspective is correct, maximizing utility subject to a budget constraint is a meaningless concept and certainly not a legitimate basis for a theory of consumer behavior.

An incorrect inference from Maslow's theory is that one must first be economically successful before being able to attempt creative outlets. This clearly is not the case, since many great works of art as well as significant inventions have occurred under conditions of poverty or near poverty. A correct inference is that at extreme levels of economic misfortune, achieving higher levels of need, including creativity, becomes increasingly difficult and less likely.

As soon as needs rather than wants become the primary focus, some type of hierarchy logically emerges. Most mainstream economists regard such rankings as inherently subjective and, therefore, unscientific. As a result, they have tended to avoid and discredit any hierarchy. Psychologists, most of whom feel more comfortable working with a hierarchy of needs, point out that satisfaction of a need in one category is in no way comparable to satisfaction of a need in another category. Being well-fed is not the same as feeling high self esteem. Clearly, this line of thinking represents a more advanced and more realistic conception of consumer behavior than one where satisfaction of all wants is reduced to a single common denominator: utility.

Amazingly, for nearly half a century the economics profession largely ignored what Maslow and other psychologists were saying about consumer behavior. Instead, mainstream economists used increasingly sophisticated mathematics in an attempt to quantify increasingly complex utility functions which, with calculus, were easily "maximized subject to a budget constraint." (Remember that utility cannot be measured and that the concept of the rational economic person is deficient, if not fraudulent!). How meaningful could this research possibly be?

Recent Research

A growing number of economists have belatedly recognized the folly of this misplaced precision.[12] Especially during the past three decades, psychologists and economists have begun working together on group research projects dealing with areas of interest to both professions.[13] In the newly emerging field of *economic psychology,* research teams have tackled such topics as psychological motives for charitable giving and for savings patterns, attitudes toward affluence in rich vs. poor countries, and psychological effects of economic events such as job loss.

Recent studies have also examined the relationship between such variables as self-image and compulsive buying, consumer satisfaction and brand-name products, behavioral problems in children and their attitudes toward materialism, and perceptions of those who have attained affluence by entrepreneurial activity versus inheritance. Much of this research is being undertaken by people who are not institutional economists and who may even embrace some mainstream dogma. The role that institutional economics has played in the debate over the relevance of psychology to economics, however, has been substantial and is well documented.[14]

Since the 1980s, *some* members of the mainstream have moved away from strict emphasis on marginal change, completely rational consumers, greed as the principal motivator, and equilibrium. The mainstream, however, has remained preoccupied with technique over substance.[15] One increasingly popular area of research has been *behavioral economics*, although even some of its proponents advertise that it tends only to "modify one or two assumptions in standard theory".[16] Models in this area have been built under assumptions that consumers use rules of thumb in making decisions, that there are bounds or limits to their rationality, and that they do exhibit "non-selfish" motives including concern for others. Other behavioral patterns sometimes considered include habits, loss aversion, and the tendencies of people to copy the behavior of others or to be inept at computation, especially probabilities. This long overdue change of focus still downplays the influence of evolutionary economists and claims an intellectual heritage largely drawn from the neoclassical school.

Many economists today even recognize an area of study called *happiness research*, which examines how economic factors like unemployment or inflation and institutional factors like type of democracy influence how satisfied people are.[17] Among their more important findings are: no correlation between wealth and happiness as well as no relationship between utility and happiness.

The development of humanistic psychology has inspired a similar specialty of *humanistic economics*. The latter has replaced utilitarianism with Maslow's hierarchy of needs and constructed a branch of the discipline that considers human development as well as economic growth.[18]

Exactly where all of this will lead remains to be seen. In an evolutionary process, the outcome is never certain. An economics discipline that has begun to focus on actual (rather than artificially contrived) people, however, cannot help but be a positive step.

Finally, there is some evidence of a renewed interest in studying Veblen's original approach to psychology, including his use of instincts. Much research has recently appeared in several different disciplines that support and reaffirm Veblen's instinct-based approach to human behavior. Together, these disciplines have come to be known as *cognitive science*, formally defined as the interdisciplinary scientific study of the mind. Its component disciplines include experimental psychology, evolutionary psychology, neuroscience, and artificial intelligence.[19]

Some of this research argues that the human brain consists of *modules,* or areas with specialized functions. These modules have been identified as essentially the same as instincts.[20] Both direct human behavior. More than one hundred currently specified modules include several that have parallels in instinct-inspired institutional economics. Taken together, tool use and appreciation of skill, for example, are virtually equivalent to the instinct of workmanship. Other modules recently labeled in cognitive science as curiosity, parenting, and pursuit of status also have a familiar Veblenian ring. Similar advances in evolutionary biology, as well as in neuroscience, draw on Veblen's notion of "purposive human behavior."[21]

Among the positions taken in this new body of research are the following:[22] The mind is a collection of modules, or what might be called smaller (less mindful) minds. Higher order brain functions such as reasoning evolve from lower-level instincts and habits to form a *cognitive ladder.* Its various steps begin with basic feedback mechanisms (reflexes or tropisms), which provide the foundation for purposeful activity (instincts), which lead to more complex thought patterns (habits) from which learning becomes possible. Finally, from these habits, higher-order capabilities, including reasoning, calculation, and judgment evolve. The pattern may be illustrated as a continual, aggregative process:

tropisms ➔ instincts ➔ habits ➔ judgment (intelligence)

In other words, the mind gets its power from a variety of different mechanisms or specialized circuits. One study even argues that "evidence is growing for the existence of learning instincts and reasoning instincts."[23] The mind uses propensities such as these to plot its next course of action. Rather than passively absorbing information from its surroundings, the mind actually creates information for its own use. The outlook for further developments in this area is promising. Clearly, instincts (even if some current professionals prefer to call them modules) have reemerged as potentially motivating forces in modern social science.

Veblen's view was that instincts and institutions influence human behavior. It has recently been argued that, in advancing this position, he reached a conclusion consistent with contemporary psychoanalytic theory.[24] Following Freud (one of his contemporaries), Veblen introduced emotions and the subconscious into economic analysis. Many of Veblen's disciples make the point that consumers do not follow *rules of thumb* and are not always rational. Unlike mainstream economists, who have simply assumed rationality without empirical proof, psychologists have actually observed human behavior and have offered empirical verification that, to the surprise of no one except perhaps mainstream economists, *people are sometimes irrational.*

Some economists[25] have recently reexamined the role played by emotions in influencing economic choice. One has argued that ". . . logic (rationality) and emotion (feeling and evaluation) constitute a nexus. It makes no sense to speak of balancing emotion and rationality when rationality is about implementing emotions."[26] In studying how emotions and the unconscious influence human behavior, for example, one contemporary psychologist has concluded that instincts are "unconsciously motivating forces" and "the center of the psychoanalytic consideration of motivation."[27] This argument suggests that instincts may be a basis for human (consumer?) behavior, even though the vast majority of psychologists today still reject instinct psychology. Most contemporary psychologists, however, accept the view that the mind is capable of being irrational. They therefore dismiss the rationality assumption of mainstream economics and are open to considering a wide range of variables that might influence consumer choice.

Drawing on the above research in psychology and in economics, some economists have recently argued that institutions can modify and even control instincts.[28] In other words, the mind's restlessness, fantasy, and irrationality lead to unpredictable behavior. Instincts may produce impulsive action, along with untamed and unreasoning tendencies. All of a sudden, impulse buying, ruled out by the rationality assumption, becomes a realistic possibility. So does the fact that consumers are not one-dimensional maximizers who may now consume for reasons other than higher levels of utility.

Research in psychology shows that it is misleading to "conceptualize people as attempting to maximize stable, coherent, and accurately perceived preferences."[29] Biologists have also developed models of human behavior that reject the rationality assumption and enable "one to provide a systematic account of observed behavior that, from a rational choice perspective, tend to be classified as unexplainable anomalies."[30] Freed from the past-binding tradition of unrealistic assumptions, contemporary economists are now able to study what *really* motivates consumers. Along with research efforts in the newly emerging field of economic psychology, Veblen and the influence of the long-suspect instinct theory may offer a place to begin.

The message for those exploring consumer behavior today is clear. Economists must be more interdisciplinary and must consider psychological, biological, social, and ethical constraints on the consumer.[31] Even economic anthropology and the biological theory of evolution, both of which played a role in Veblen's evolutionary economics, merit close reconsideration.[32] Despite the voluminous research discrediting the assumptions and the psychology upon which the discipline of economics has been based, mainstream economists continue to build more elaborate models upon these false premises without so much as even acknowledging that this dissent exists.

The theory of consumer behavior is far more complicated than mainstream economics has led us to believe. People obviously consume for reasons more complex than a desire to maximize utility or anything else. The challenge for those attempting to develop a more realistic theory of consumer behavior is to identify these multiple, interdisciplinary factors and articulate their importance more persuasively than mainstream economists have presented their case for over a century. Institutional reluctance to change, even within the economics profession, has once again proven to be a formidable force in countering the advance of knowledge and human progress.

Veblen no doubt would have viewed unrealistic assumptions in economic models as imbecile institutions. They fit all the necessary requirements to be designated as such. They are past binding, resistant to change, an established way of doing things, and yes, even ceremonial in nature.

Footnotes:

1. Geoffrey M. Hodgson, "The Approach of Institutional Economics," *Journal of Economic Literature,* 36, 1 (March 1998), p. 189.

2. Thorstein Veblen, "Why Is Economics Not an Evolutionary Science?" in *The Place of Science in Modern Civilization,* (New York: B. W. Huebsch, 1919), pp. 73–74.

3. Tetsuo Taka, "The Place of Economic Man in Evolutionary Economics: Veblen and Commons Reconsidered," *Annals of the Society for the History of Economic Thought,* 44, 4 (November 2003), pp. 17–30.

4. Hans E. Jensen, "The Theory of Human Nature," *Journal of Economic Issues,* 21, 3 (September 1987), p. 1069.

5. Robert T. Averitt, "Review of *Institutional Economics,* by Wendell Gordon," *Journal of Economic Issues,* 15, 4 (December 1981), p. 1043.

6. When, as a young man, Clarence Ayres was invited to

dinner at the home of Thorstein Veblen in 1920, Veblen asked: "Ayres, do you remember how I defined 'instincts'?" After a long pause, Ayres replied: "No, I don't." It was the right answer. Veblen never gave a formal definition and said so to Ayres at this meeting. See Joseph E. Pluta, "The Last Course on Institutionalism Taught by Clarence E. Ayres," *Research in the History of Economic Thought and Methodology, 26B* (2008), pp. 309-336. The story is also recalled in Rick Tilman, *The Intellectual Legacy of Thorstein Veblen: Unresolved Issues,* (London: Greenwood Press, 1996), p. 106, fn. 46.

7. Pier Francesco Asso and Luca Fiorito, "Human Nature and Economic Institutions: Instinct Psychology, Behaviorism, and the Development of American Institutionalism," *Journal of the History of Economic Thought,* 26, 4 (December 2004), pp. 445–477.

8. Tilman, p. 99. Chapter 3, entitled "Veblen's Psychology and Its Doctrinal Roots," contains much valuable background on instincts including the works of William McDougall, C. Lloyd Morgan, Jacques Loeb, and William James. All were noted psychologists and/or philosophers who influenced Veblen.

9. Charles G. Leathers, "Veblen and Hayek on Instincts and Evolution," *Journal of the History of Economic Thought,* 12, 2 (Fall 1990), p. 163.

10. Mark A. Lutz and Kenneth Lux, *The Challenge of Humanistic Economics,* (Menlo Park, CA: Benjamin/ Cummings, 1979).

11. Abraham Maslow, *Motivation and Personality,* (New York: Harper and Row, 1954).

12. John M. Gowdy and Raluca Iorgulescu Polimeni, "The

Death of Homo Economicus: Is There Life after Welfare Economics?" *International Journal of Social Economics,* 32, 11 (2005), pp. 924–938.

13. Esther-Mirjam Sent, "Behavioral Economics: How Psychology Made Its (Limited) Way Back into Economics," *History of Political Economy,* 36, 3 (Winter 2004), pp. 735–760.

14. Shira B. Lewin, "Economics and Psychology: Lessons for Our Own Day from the Early Twentieth Century," *Journal of Economic Literature,* 34, 3 (September 1996), pp. 1293–1323.

15. Geoffrey M. Hodgson, "Evolutionary and Institutional Economics as the New Mainstream?" *Evolutionary and Institutional Economic Review,* 4, 1 (2007), pp. 7-25.

16. Colin Camerer, George Lowenstein, and Mathew Rabin, eds., *Advances in Behavioral Economics,* (Princeton, NJ: Princeton University Press, 2004), p. 2. For a short introduction to the topic, see Hugh Schwartz, *A Guide to Behavioral Economics*, (Falls Church, Virginia: Higher Education Publications, 2008). For a more advanced analysis, see Stefano Della Vigna, "Psychology and Economics: Evidence from the Field." *Journal of Economic Literature*, 47, 2 (June 2009): pp. 315–72.

17. Richard A. Easterlin, "The Economics of Happiness," *Daedalus* 49, 1 (Spring 2004), pp. 26–33. See also Bruno S. Frey and Alois Stutzer, "Happiness Research: State and Prospects," *Review of Social Economy,* 63, 2 (June 2005), pp. 207–228.

18. George P. Brockway, *The End of Economic Man: An Introduction to Humanistic Economics,* (New York: W.W.

Norton, 2001).

19. Paul Twomey, "Reviving Veblenian Economic Psychology," *Cambridge Journal of Economics,* 22, 4 (July 1998), pp. 433–448.

20. William H. Redmond, "Instinct, Culture, and Cognitive Science," *Journal of Economic Issues,* 40, 2 (June 2006), pp. 431–438.

21. Michael S. Lawlor, "William James's Psychological Pragmatism: Habit, Belief, and Purposive Human Behavior," *Cambridge Journal of Economics,* 30, 3 (May 2006), pp. 321–345.

22. See Twomey, pp. 438–445, especially where he is summarizing the results found in Leda Cosmides and John Tooby, "Better than Rational: Evolutionary Psychology and the Invisible Hand," *American Economic Review,* 84, 2 (May 1994), pp. 327–332; Stan Franklin, *Artificial Minds,* (Cambridge, MA: MIT Press, 1995); and Howard Margolis, *Patterns, Thinking and Cognition: A Theory of Judgment,* (Chicago: University of Chicago Press, 1987).

23. Twomey, p. 443.

24. Harold Wolozin, "Thorstein Veblen and Human Emotions: An Unfulfilled Prescience," *Journal of Economic Issues,* 39, 3 (September 2005), pp. 727–740.

25. Jon Elster, "Emotions and Economic Theory," *Journal of Economic Literature,* 36, 1 (March, 1998), pp. 47–74.

26. A. Allan Schmid, *Conflict and Cooperation: Institutional and Behavioral Economics,* (Malden, MA: Blackwell

Publishing, 2004), p. 36.

27. Hans W. Loewald, *Papers on Psychoanalysis,* (New Haven, CT: Yale University Press, 1980), p. 109, quoted in Wolozin, p. 734.

28. Wolozin, pp. 738–739. Other contemporary institutional economists prefer that emphasis be given to habits instead of instincts. See, for example, Tilman, p. 102 and Hodgson, p. 169. Tilman, a leading Veblen scholar, argues, for example, that habit "is the key to Veblen's social psychology."

29. Matthew Rabin, "Psychology and Economics," *Journal of Economic Literature,* 36, 1 (March 1998), pp. 11–46.

30. Viktor Vanberg, "The Rationality Postulate in Economics: Its Ambiguity, Its Deficiency, and Its Evolutionary Alternative," *Journal of Economic Methodology,* 11, 1 (March 2004), p. 12.

31. Charles G. Leathers and J. Patrick Raines, "Veblen's Evolutionary Economics of Religion and the Evolutionary Psychology of Religion", *International Journal of Social Economics*, 41, 2 (2014), pp. 146-161; G. R. Steele, "Understanding Economic Man: Psychology, Rationality, and Values," *American Journal of Economics and Sociology,* 63, 4 (November 2004), pp. 1021–1029; and Felipe Almeida, "Thorstein Veblen and Albert Bandura: A Modern Psychological Reading of the Conspicuous Consumer", *Journal of Economic Issues*, 48, 1 (March 2014), pp. 109-122.

32. Tetsuo Taka, "Veblen's Theory of Evolution and the Instinct of Workmanship: An Ethological and Biological Reinterpretation," *The History of Economic Thought,* 47, 2 (December 2005), pp. 32–44.

Chapter Five

Myrdal and Ayres on the Path to Progress

The key reason executives are paid so much now is that they appoint the members of the corporate board that determines their compensation....So it's not the invisible hand of the market that leads to those monumental executive incomes; it's the invisible handshake in the boardroom.

Paul Krugman

The striking thing about America is that productivity of workers and wages have not moved in tandem.

Joseph Stiglitz

Production functions involving only land, labor, and capital....never work and never explain economic development.

Kenneth E. Boulding

Building upon the insights of both David Ricardo and the nineteenth century marginalists, mainstream economists today still venerate the law of diminishing returns. Briefly stated, as a firm combines more of a variable input (such as labor) with a fixed input (such as land), eventually increases in output become smaller. Like death and taxes, diminishing returns are presumed to be inevitable; they are supposedly a part of every production process. Examples of this principle are especially evident in agriculture and manufacturing, although they exist elsewhere as well. Adding workers to a fixed number of machines adequately achieves the desired supporting result. An often cited "proof" is that, if the law did not hold, the world's food supply could be grown in a flower pot. Thus, the validity of the law is easily supported.

Graphical analysis provides us with the three stages of production in which the first demonstrates increasing returns to the variable input, the second diminishing returns, and the third negative returns. Because of a mirror image relationship, cost curves similarly illustrate diminishing returns (increasing costs) when marginal and average costs eventually rise.

Production analysis provides the quintessential answer to the question of how managers determine the optimal mix of labor and machinery. When a soft drink producer, for example, wants to increase its daily output of bottled cola, it can achieve its goal by either hiring an additional worker (L) or machine (K). On what basis should management logically choose between them?

First, the amounts that another worker and another machine add to total output (bottles of cola) would need to be considered. Of course, today's highly sophisticated bottling machines easily produce more than a worker. But that is only half the picture because the machine undoubtedly costs considerably more than the wage paid to the worker. Added output per added input cost is what guides the choice. Management, therefore, would probably reason something like the following: how much additional output (MP_K) would the machine contribute in relation to its cost (P_K) versus how much additional output (MP_L) would the laborer contribute in relation to his/her cost (P_L)? The notation P_K represents the price of a machine, while P_L represents the price of labor, more commonly called the wage. If MP_K/P_K is greater than MP_L/P_L, then clearly the machine should be hired instead of the worker. However, if MP_K/P_K is less than MP_L/P_L, then the worker should be hired instead of the machine. Where does this reasoning logically lead?

To make the most efficient use of productive inputs,

workers and machines should be hired up to the point where

$$MP_K/P_K = MP_L/P_L$$

This formula shows how one determines the optimal number of machines and workers in any production facility. The formula advises that inputs should be hired up to the point where their marginal product to price ratios are equal. At this point, the cost of producing a given output is lowest. This formula is sometimes referred to as the *rule for optimal combination of inputs.*

There are several ways in which this rule might be considered. One example may hit especially close to home. Does the university you attend hire the best faculty available? Using this formula, the answer is (sadly): NO. It hires the best faculty it can afford. It considers, in other words, not only the additional output the faculty member can contribute (MP_L), but also how much he or she will cost (P_L). A school with limited resources (or with short-sighted, penny-pinching administrators) must hire whomever is left after those schools that place a high priority on quality faculty have already selected those professors with the highest MP_L.

Technological Change

In the short run, when the law of diminishing returns applies, firms can increase output only by adding more of a variable input (labor) to the fixed input (capital or the size of plant). This limited possible producer response to price changes means that supply is relatively inelastic. In the long run, all inputs, including plant size, can vary and the only limit on output is technology. The greater possibility for producer response to price changes means that supply is relatively elastic.

In the historical period, technological change occurs

and the productivity of both workers and machines rises. Because possible producer response to price changes has increased substantially, supply becomes highly elastic and innovation generates products only dreamed of in earlier periods. Because of technological change, the production function or total product curve shifts upward.[1] As a result, more output can be produced with each amount of labor than was previously the case. Labor productivity has, therefore, risen as has the productive capacity of the firm.

From the Industrial Revolution in the eighteenth century when steam power and other inventions revolutionized production processes to twenty-first-century advances in scientific and medical technology, output in thousands of firms has mushroomed, new businesses and new jobs have been created, new products have emerged, and living standards have risen. The technique of production analysis has enabled some quantification of the most dramatic of these changes. Throughout much of the twentieth century, technological progress, growth in the stock of capital, and higher educational and skill levels have had the most profound effects on the American standard of living.

Some Technical Issues

Neoclassical economists in the nineteenth century used the concept of marginal productivity to challenge the view of Karl Marx that workers are exploited and to argue that each worker is paid exactly what he or she deserves. While most people today would agree that a heart surgeon contributes more to society than the person who sweeps the floors, few contemporary economists believe that every single worker in the world is paid exactly what his or her marginal product is.

Many economists have argued that, in practice, it is often quite difficult to separate the marginal products of labor, management, and machinery. If a television manufacturer, for example, hires one additional worker and all other resources stay the same (*ceteris paribus*), then any increase in output can arguably be credited to the additional worker. If the firm, however, hires more workers, machines, and managers at the same time, how much of the output rise can be attributed to each additional resource? Similarly, are accountants more productive today than they were twenty years ago because they are better educated or because modern computer software allows forms to be completed faster? Here, the answer is probably some of both, but it is hard to say which portions are due to the marginal productivity of the accountant and the marginal productivity of the machine.

In a given circumstance, it may in fact be true that, when seeking to expand output, the manager of a firm will hire the resource whose additional productivity per dollar is higher. For example, if the choice is between one more worker and one more machine and if $MP_L/P_L > MP_K/P_K$, the worker would obviously be the better choice. How many managers, however, actually staff their operations to the point where the marginal product to price ratios are equal for *all* resources employed? This is what the mathematical properties of these relationships suggest should be done but few if any managers take the time to do this sort of calculation. Indeed, the added cost of obtaining this information may not be worth the effort, especially when many different types of labor and machinery are employed in a large corporation. When separating MP_L and MP_K is difficult as shown above, even performing the simple MP/P calculation may be impossible.

A larger issue centers on quality. Throughout this analysis, output is measured in number of physical units. General Motors may appear more productive when it increases the quantity of cars and trucks it manufactures from one year to the next. How quickly they fall apart is not considered at all. This may, in fact, be a major issue in the economic difficulty experienced by the firm and its need for federal government bailouts. The productivity of several other firms in other industries may be similarly overestimated.

Impoverished Countries

More serious critiques come from those who question the applicability of Western production analysis concepts in developing countries. Two of the most astute commentators have been British economist E. F. Schumacher and Nobel Prize–winning Swedish economist Gunnar Myrdal. Schumacher challenged the view that resource-poor countries need large amounts of advanced Western technology in order to experience economic growth. He also doubted that sophisticated growth models, including those that use a form of production analysis and treat people as merely another resource, provide the guidance that poor nations need.

In his highly influential 1973 book *Small Is Beautiful: Economics as if People Mattered,*[2] Schumacher proposed development of "intermediate technology" and greater use of the most abundant resource in Asia, Africa, and Latin America: people. Intermediate technology is more expensive than what is currently used in a developing nation but less expensive than what is prevalent in industrialized nations. It includes up-to-date agricultural implements, food-processing techniques, wind power, irrigation systems, and other environmentally friendly technologies that locals are able to repair. It can best be used if workplaces are created where people are currently living rather than in large metropolitan areas. If expensive machinery and skilled experts do not have to be imported, multiple worksites with uncomplicated production methods can be established. Production by the masses is seen as the alternative to mass production.

Myrdal, author of the 1968 classic *Asian Drama,*[3] was similarly bothered by uncritical use of Western production/

growth models in developing countries and argued for a more interdisciplinary understanding of economies and cultures in poverty-stricken regions of the world. He emphasized that labor productivity is very low in poor nations and could be enhanced by better nutrition, health care, education, and attitudes toward work. He was also concerned about the laissez faire bias of most economic analysis, when government planning, in his view, is essential to initiate and direct the development process where entrepreneurs and other resources are scarce.

Although so much of traditional microeconomics focuses on the short run, Myrdal believed that long-run considerations were more important in analyzing the growth potential of poor countries. One of the biggest long-run problems, he emphasized, was population growth which lowered both per-capita incomes and labor productivity as labor markets became flooded with low-skill workers. This ultimately meant that poor countries produced relatively few goods that other nations wished to import. In traditional production analysis, more workers supposedly result in more output, an outcome not usually achieved in poor countries where far too many workers lack adequate skills to contribute effectively in the workplace.

In developing the concept of circular and cumulative causation discussed earlier, Myrdal rejected the idea of diminishing returns to capital because increases in knowledge prevent this "law" from happening. Knowledge generated within the economic system itself gives rise to technological advance and improvements in productivity. Sources of knowledge include investment in research and development, human capital, physical capital, and learning by doing. Knowledge does not allow the marginal product of capital to diminish to the point where investment is no longer profitable. As a result, *knowledge as an input to the production process generates increasing returns rather than diminishing returns.*[4]

Production analysis may offer some insight into the impact of technological change within industrialized nations. But what if past-binding traditions and cultural taboos in poor countries pose a resistance to technical advance, modernization, and economic progress? In such cases, new technology will not have as profound an impact as production analysis would predict. Obviously, the force that opposes progress is important and merits close scrutiny.

Economists Thorstein Veblen and Clarence Ayres, both of whom were critical of mainstream microeconomic methods, included this resistance to change in their analysis. Veblen addressed this problem in his 1914 book *The Instinct of Workmanship*[5] and Ayres stated it more clearly in his 1962 edition of *The Theory of Economic Progress.*[6] Veblen and Ayres have argued that the societies that have experienced economic progress have been those where the dynamic force of change has successfully overcome the traditions, customs, myths, and habits that shun new ideas. Clearly, the opposition to modernization in much of the Middle East and to birth control in Latin America, the embrace of superstition in rural Africa, and the religious-based respect given to animals in portions of South Asia have inhibited economic advance in those regions.

Production analysis documents the beneficial effects of technological change but ignores resistance to that change rooted in the cultures of individual societies. Institutionalism places this ceremonial behavior at the center of its interdisciplinary analysis and gives a more balanced view of the forces promoting and inhibiting progress. It is also potentially more valuable in influencing policy in poor countries than an approach that views only the positive effects of new tools and human skills based on values predominant in industrialized nations.

Recent research has documented ceremonial impediments to industrial growth policies in Brazil,[7] corruption of political leaders in 39 African nations,[8] the growing preference for male children in India,[9] and the inefficient military in 19th century Russia.[10] All of these case studies show that resistance to change and established ways of doing things slow the path of progress. At the center of analysis in all of these studies, it is doubtful that, in mainstream study, these issues would have merited more than either obligatory caveat, casual mention, or brief footnote.

For nearly four decades (1930–1969), Ayres was the leading member of the department of economics at the University of Texas. Its faculty also included during this time such noted institutionalists as Robert Montgomery, E. E. Hale, Ruth Allen, Erich Zimmermann, and Wendell Gordon. Together they formed the *Texas School of Institutionalism*, a group that advanced the ideas of Veblen and applied them to problems in various fields of economics.[11]

Especially in the aftermath of World War II, institutionalist thinking contributed much to understanding the problems of developing countries where ceremonialism and superstition helped to slow the advance of technological change. Today, those ideas still more accurately describe conditions in poor regions of the world than more mathematically sophisticated models built in the neoclassical tradition.

During the 1970s, the economics department at Texas struggled to redefine its identity before finally rebuilding along mainstream lines. Most of the faculty currently teaching there have never heard of Veblen, Ayres, or institutionalism. Followers of this school of thought are now scattered among various universities across the nation where the dissent they teach still challenges mainstream thinking.

One additional institutional resistance to change in impoverished countries has recently shown signs of giving way to a novel idea capable of generating economic progress in small but effective doses. Banks in poor countries and elsewhere have traditionally resisted providing loans to those who lack adequate collateral or other evidence of credit worthiness.

In 1976, Muhammad Yunus, a university economist in famine-stricken Bangladesh, founded the Grameen Bank, which began making small loans at minimal interest rates to aspiring entrepreneurs, primarily rural women. Even though collateral is not required, more than 98 percent of Grameen Bank loans have been repaid in full. Within thirty years, *microcredit* programs were creating small business ventures in over one hundred countries, including the United States.[12] The average amount of a loan during the first twenty years of the bank's operation was $120.[13] In 2006, Yunus was awarded the Nobel Peace Prize. Long-established banking practices and the traditional role of women in several Muslim countries have also been challenged.

It should also be pointed out, however, that with the passage of time, the performance of the Grameen Bank has increasingly been questioned as an imperfect institution itself. For example, in cases where a high proportion of its loans have been secured for consumption rather than investment purposes, few jobs have been created.[14] This has apparently been most obvious in Bangladesh.

Making Goods versus Making Money

In the United States today, top executives in major corporations often receive salaries that are dozens, and in some cases even hundreds, of times greater than salaries earned by assembly-line production workers. Marginal productivity theory justifies these enormous wage differentials on grounds that the first group is supposedly that much more productive than the second.

Such claims are especially weak in instances where top-level executives award themselves sizable bonuses when the firm's profit level as well as stock price drop and assembly-line workers are either laid off or asked to take salary cuts. Performance measures, in other words, indicate a lack of productivity on the part of management which is then rewarded for its ineptness.

Veblen saw no value in a marginal productivity theory that justified huge salary discrepancies based on supposed productivity differences, which at best could not be measured accurately and which at worst did not exist. The distinction he saw was between those who were making goods (*industrial pursuits*) and those who were making money (*pecuniary activities*).[15] Actual production of goods was carried on by engineers, designers, craftsmen, assembly-line workers, mechanics, and so forth. Pecuniary activities were carried on by advertisers, middle managers, corporate lawyers and accountants, as well as others. This latter group, along with most top-level managers, *did not produce anything* but merely engaged in marketing already existing products, negotiations, merger overtures, financial matters, and public relations.

In early industrial America and even in some small businesses today, owner-managers and production employees worked side by side. This hands-on management style increased the likelihood of high-quality products and kept top-level people in the loop insofar as knowing what was going on in the production process. Some of these business owners designed the product itself and even built the machines used in its manufacture. Veblen respectfully called such managers *captains of industry* to denote their leadership roles in instructing workers in the craft of the enterprise.

As smaller businesses grow into corporate behemoths, however, the top-level managerial function effectively splits from production activities. Eventually, various groups within the firm become more interested in clever image ploys, creative accounting, and financial manipulations than in genuine product improvement. The captains of industry, in effect, evolve into *captains of finance* who have virtually nothing to do with the manufacture of the product. Evolutionary economists might even go so far as to say that *marginal productivity theory explains nothing in a setting in which some of the highest-paid people produce nothing.*

Those who genuflect at the altar of the market continue to use the marginal productivity theory to justify huge differences in income and wealth. Many also assert, without proof, that any movement toward a more equal income and wealth distribution would destroy work incentives and thereby undermine the market system, bringing economic expansion to a halt. One of the more insightful challenges to this position is the following:

> A highly skewed distribution of income is detrimental to the development of the type of broadbased consumerism that buoyed the United States economy in the post-1945 era. It is questionable whether the "golden age" (1945–1972) expansion of output and productive capacity could have been achieved without the ameliorative effects of the minimum wage, unionism and collective bargaining, progressive taxation, and income transfers.[16]

Implications

One of the most serious issues affecting the American economy since the 1980s has been the decline and impending disappearance of the middle class. This has been caused in part by huge salaries paid to top level managers while wages paid to workers have increased only slightly. Such earnings differentials cannot possibly be explained by differences in productivity. Justification given by many mainstream economists using productivity data are little short of laughable.

The perspectives of Schumacher, Myrdal, Veblen, and Ayres help to give a more complete picture of issues surrounding production and growth. Despite their reservations, the strongest of which apply in the case of developing countries, production analysis is still widely used in industrialized nations today where statistics on productivity, if not MP/P ratios, presumably influence managerial decision making. Decisions based on poor measures cannot possibly contribute to any standard of efficiency or to any indicator of progress.

Footnotes:

1. The concept and mainstream reasoning derived from it have recently been thoroughly criticized. See J. Felipe and J. S. L. McCombie, "The Aggregate Production Function: 'Not Even Wrong'", *Review of Political Economy*, 26, 1, (2014), pp. 60-84 and Robert P. Murphy, "Interest and the Marginal Product of Capital: A Critique of Samuelson", *Journal of the History of Economic Thought*, 29, 4 (December 2007), pp. 453-464.

2. E. F. Schumacher, *Small Is Beautiful: Economics As If People Mattered,* (New York: Harper and Row, 1973).

3. Gunnar Myrdal, *Asian Drama: An Inquiry into the Poverty of Nations,* (Harmondsworth: Penguin,1968).

4. Phillip Toner, *Main Currents in Cumulative Causation: The Dynamics of Growth and Development,* (London: Macmillan Press, 1999), pp. 165–168. The inevitability of diminishing returns has also been challenged in other areas, including international trade by, among others, a Nobel Prize winning

economist. See Paul Krugman, "The Increasing Returns Revolution in Trade and Geography." *American Economic Review*, 99, 3 (May 2009), pp. 561–71. The likelihood of increasing returns in the development of modern computer technology is illustrated in W. Bryan Arthur, “Increasing Returns and the New World of Business,” *Harvard Business Review,* 74, 4 (July/August 1996), p. 100.

5. Thorstein Veblen, *The Instinct of Workmanship and the State of the Industrial Arts,* (New York: Viking Press, 1914).

6. Clarence Ayres, *The Theory of Economic Progress,* 2nd ed., (New York: Schocken Books, 1962).

7. James M. Cypher, “Emerging Contradictions of Brazil’s Neo-Developmentalism: Precarious Growth, Redistribution, and Deindustrialization”, *Journal of Economic Issues*, 49, 3 (September 2015), pp. 617-648; Rafael R. Ioris and Antonio A. R. Aoris, “The Brazilian Developmentalist State in Historical Perspective: Revisiting the 1950s in Light of Today’s Challenges”, *Journal of Iberian and Latin American Research*, 19, 1 (July 2013), pp. 133-148; and Susanna B. Hecht, “The New Amazon Geographies, Insurgent Citizenship, ‘Amazon Nation’, and the Politics of Environmentalisms”, *Journal of Cultural Geography*, 28, 1 (February 2011), pp. 203-223.

8. Uchenna Efobi, “Politicians’ Attributes and Institutional Quality in Africa: A Focus on Corruption”, *Journal of Economic Issues*, 49, 3 (September 2015), pp. 787-813; Jacob W. Musila, “Does Democracy Have a Different Impact on Corruption in Africa?” *Journal of African Business*, 14, 3 (September 2013), pp. 162-170; and Herbert Werlin, “Understanding International Corruption and What to Do About It”, *Challenge*, 56, 3 (May 2013), pp.53-73.

9. Aparna Mitra, "Son Preference in India: Implications for Gender Development", *Journal of Economic Issues*, 48, 4 (December 2014), pp. 1021-1037; D. P. Chaudhri and Raghbendra Jha, "India's Gender Bias in Child Population, Female Education and Growing Prosperity, 1951-2011", *International Review of Applied Economics,* 27, 1 (January 2013), pp. 23-43; and Susmita Bharati et. al., "Is Son Preference Pervasive in India?" *Journal of Gender Studies*, 20, 3 (September 2011), pp. 291-298.

10. Alexander Maslov and Vyachislav Volchik, "Institutions and Lagging Development: The Case of the Don Army Region", *Journal of Economic Issues*, 48, 3 (September 2014), pp. 727-742.

11. Daniel Morgan, "Ayres and Hale in Texas 1950s", *Journal of Economic Issues*, 48, 4 (December 2014), pp. 1169-1170 and Ronnie J. Phillips, "Is There a 'Texas School' of Economics?" *Journal of Economic Issues,* 23, 3 (September 1989), pp. 863–872.

12. "Banking on the Poor Makes Economic Sense," *The Boston Globe,* (October 18, 2006); Berhanu Nega and Geoffrey Schneider, "Social Entrepreneurship, Microfinance, and Economic Development in Africa", *Journal of Economic Issues*, 48, 2 (June 2014), pp. 367-376; and Tonia Warnecke, "The 'Individualist Entrepreneur' vs. Socially Sustainable Development: Can Microfinance Build Community?" *Journal of Economic Issues*, 48, 2 (June 2014), pp. 377-386.

13. Alexandra Bernasek and James Ronald Stanfield, "The Grameen Bank as Progressive Institutional Adjustment," *Journal of Economic Issues,* 31, 2 (June 1997), pp. 359–366.

14. Rafiqul Islam Molla, M. Mahmudul Alam, and Abu N. M.

Wahid, "Questioning Bangladesh's Microcredit", *Challenge*, 51, 6 (November-December 2008), pp. 113-121.

15. Veblen originally proposed this distinction in *The Theory of Business Enterprise,* 1904, especially chapters 2 and 3. His arguments are nicely summarized in Charles Sachrey, Geoffrey Schneider, and Janet Knoedler, *Introduction to Political Economy,* 4th ed., (Boston: Economic Affairs Bureau, 2005), pp. 95–97.

16. Christopher Brown, "Is There an Institutional Theory of Distribution?" *Journal of Economic Issues,* 39, 4 (December 2005), p. 926.

Chapter Six

The Fictions of Pure Competition and Value Free Economics

Economics has never been a science and it is even less now than a few years ago.

Paul Samuelson

Economists themselves, like most specialists, normally suffer from a kind of metaphysical blindness, assuming that theirs is a science of absolute and invariable truths, without any presuppositions.

E. F. Schumacher

Farming looks mighty easy when your plow is a pencil and you are a thousand miles from the corn field.

Dwight D. Eisenhower

Mainstream economists have had a long love affair with pure competition. In their valiant effort to turn fiction into reality, various products have been cleverly modified to fit more readily into this imaginative theoretical box. The still short list of items that might be produced under conditions nearing this "competitive ideal" includes a number of agricultural products (corn, wheat, eggs, rice, potatoes, and the like), some species of fish (cod?), and even early computer disks. Other products which stretch the mind a bit but may still "resemble" this market structure include stock exchanges, the (nearly) identical products of street vendors, and contract construction, the latter because it is standardized in its mass produced frame houses and low quality workmanship. All of these examples have appeared in microeconomic principles texts.

One of the more unusual, clearly tongue in cheek, claims of a purely competitive output is the trinket. A trinket may be defined as "a totally useless object, such as a wedding gift or holiday present that gathers dust in the closet for years because it has no known practical value but cannot be discarded because such an action might hurt the feelings of the distant relative who did not think enough of you to buy you something useful in the first place."[1] Trinkets are most often sold by stores euphemistically known as gift shops.

Justifications for this abstraction from common sense have produced a number of cute illustrations, including the following story.[2] A young man and his significant other go on a picnic. They find a romantic spot with a spectacular hillside view of a lake, spread a blanket, uncork a bottle of wine, and begin eating sandwiches from their picnic basket. As a few crumbs drop on the blanket, an uninvited third party arrives: ants. His immediate first reaction might be to stomp on the intruders, curse, spill the wine, and generally destroy this magnificent moment. Assuming the crumbs were few in number, a more rational approach might be to sit back, watch the ants devour their snack, and then see what happens. Finding no additional food, the ants are likely to leave peacefully and seek munchies elsewhere.

In this little allegory, the crumbs are economic profits and the ants are (roughly equal sized? small? typical? "representative"?) firms. When crumbs (and profits) are plentiful, ants (and new firms) are attracted. When crumbs (and profits) vanish, there is no threat that ants (or firms) will enter the scene. Ease of entry and exit is presumably reinforced by this semi-literary diversion. Of course, in the world of business, the fierce competition for profit is no picnic.

A more succinct statement, built on the need to have a standard with which other market settings are compared, might even be offered. Pure competition is like virginity or an honest politician. Although all three may be rare in practice, they must be clearly understood before alternative forms of behavior are objectively evaluated.

The concept is difficult to teach with a straight face. Students are more likely to continue listening after a healthy-sized anesthetic of humor has been delivered. Given the subject matter, a class may have difficulty telling when jest has ended and seriousness has begun.

Welcome to the Land of Milk and Honey

There is an old saying that beauty is in the eye of the beholder. Two different people, for example, may view the same work of abstract art with noticeably different emotions. The first may admire the painting for hours, marvel at its complex array of colors, and even share the anguish felt by the artist. The second may think the painting was the canvas where house painters cleaned their brushes.

Because they see beauty in efficiency, mainstream economists view long-run equilibrium in pure competition as genuinely beautiful. In this obviously misguided sense of grandeur, both allocative (P = MC) and technical (P = AC) efficiency are alleged to be present. The former means, first of all, that resources are attracted to their best possible uses and competition forces an industry to produce an output consumers most prefer. Price measures the worth of the product to the consumer at the margin and MC is what measures the opportunity cost to society of producing the last unit of the product. In other words, price measures the benefit to the consumer of the last unit to be produced while MC measures the sacrifices of other products that have to be made for that last unit to be produced.

When $P > MC$, consumers are sacrificing more at the margin to buy the good than the value of other products they might buy. The industry is not producing as much of the product as consumers prefer. When $P < MC$, the opposite occurs. The industry is producing more of the product than consumers prefer, in terms of the sacrifice of alternative goods. Producing where $P = MC$ leads to equality between the degree to which the consumer values the product and the degree to which the consumer values alternative products. In other words, the composition of output is that which consumers most prefer.

Allocative efficiency is significant for yet another reason. When $P = MC$, the price the consumer pays for a product is just equal to the marginal (or additional) cost of producing that very unit the consumer buys. If, for example, you pay $50 for a small table (assuming it is produced under conditions of long-run equilibrium in pure competition), the price you pay is just equal to the additional cost the firm incurred to produce that very table. As a consumer, it would be difficult for you to get a better deal. The firm can do this, of course, because a normal profit is included in the firm's cost. So the firm is earning just enough to stay in business.

Mainstream technical efficiency tells us that the goods consumers want are produced in the least costly manner or that the physical use of resources is minimized. Not only is $P = AC$, but $P =$ the lowest possible AC. The minimum point on the long-run average total cost curve is also considered the point of full capacity, the level of production that can be achieved at the lowest per-unit cost with the optimal plant. If the firm produced less, it would be operating with excess capacity or wasted space.

Under technical efficiency, therefore, the price paid by the consumer is just equal to the lowest possible unit cost of production in a plant that is fully utilizing its available space. In addition, the cost curves need only include production costs. Since products are standardized, there are no selling or advertising costs which the consumer would ultimately have to pay.

Finally, the competitive ideal allegedly achieves results consistent with the interests of consumers and producers. Both groups seek to minimize the opportunity costs of making their utility maximizing and profit-maximizing choices, respectively. Society as a whole benefits if output expands to the point at which the additional benefits to consumers and the additional costs to producers are equal. In technical terms, this means that all of the consumer surplus and producer surplus[3] are realized. This results in maximum benefits to society as a whole.

In long run equilibrium in pure competition, therefore, nirvana is reached, everything is beautiful, and no alternative solution could possibly be better for anyone. The world has achieved pure bliss and the religious belief that people can only be completely happy in the next world has been seriously challenged.

Ideal vs. Real

In their enthusiasm to see their work blessed by no less an authority than Adam Smith, neoclassical economists over the years have exaggerated Smith's appreciation for and alleged endorsement of the equilibrium concept. In fact, Smith never supported equilibrium as his model of choice. He merely observed a tendency of market prices to gravitate toward a "natural price." Rather than equilibrium, his major concern was explaining the dynamic process of economic growth. In *The Wealth of Nations,* the central role he gives to the division of labor, the accumulation of capital, and the institutions necessary to create wealth make his major work more of an evolutionary study than a static one.[4] Mainstream economists have conveniently, and perhaps cleverly, chosen to ignore Smith's wider vision in favor of an equilibrium notion to which he devotes at best minor attention.

A leading institutional economist, Edythe S. Miller, has recently provided a succinct statement of the focus of institutionalism and its differences with mainstream thought. Since pure or ideal competition represents the logical apex of mainstream reasoning on the beneficial effects of market outcomes, her comments capture the evolutionary position on the neoclassical methods described above:

> The view of economic direction as one of movement—impelled by disturbances—from equilibrium to equilibrium is a distorted and incorrect perspective. Society and the economy do not gravitate toward defined "states of rest" nor toward ideal structures. The economic process is continuous and unbounded. Means are selected to achieve particular ends that themselves become means to further ends. . . . *There are no final ends in life lived in real time.* The fact of movement is inevitable; the direction of movement is unspecified. Moreover, selected goals may not be achieved. . . . If achieved, they may not meet expectations. . . .
>
> Institutional economics is realistic and deals with the matter-of-fact. . . . The productivity that is the province of industry for the most part enhances human well being. Profit seeking has the potential for harm. . . . Such actions are possible because of the possession by certain entities of market power.[5]

There is no role for power in the competitive ideal.

The firm is representative, or typical, of all firms in the industry. They are all supposedly of relatively equal (small) size and no one firm can influence market price. This scenario may have described to some extent circumstances at the time of Adam Smith's England (late 18th century). In recent years, even the most highly competitive industries include some firms with more market power (ability to influence price) than others.

Evolutionary economists criticize the characteristics of pure competition as unrealistic or even fictional. Mainstream research supporting the existence of industries that fit this model has been scant at best. The efficiency standards of ideal competition, however, are still nostalgically cherished by those who defend the neoclassical position.

Miller goes on to highlight major features in the research agenda of evolutionary economists and suggests that their policy recommendations are open to various interpretations but certainly are not based on achieving some pre-specified ideal state:

> Institutionalists perceive the purpose behind economic research as an increased understanding of how our economic world works so as to improve the potential for the identification and resolution of economic problems. . . . Institutionalism postulates experimentation to find the correct fit between problem and solution. . . .
>
> The purpose of experimentation is to confirm or disprove the usefulness and suitability of specific programs and policies for problem solution. Nor should policies adopted be taken as once and for all solutions. For institutionalism also recognizes that solutions

> to problems may be time and situation dependent—what works at one time and place, for one set of circumstances, should not in a changing economy be expected to work for all time. But at bottom, institutionalism maintains that public policies need be evaluated . . . not in terms of their adherence to an ideal, but in terms of their consequences for the public good.[6]

These statements directly challenge the mainstream position that at least some industries come close to the competitive ideal or that government policy, when it must be undertaken, should be based on strategies that move a given industry closer to that ideal. The mainstream views experimentation as tinkering with market outcomes that are best left alone.

Equilibrium and natural law were derived from scientific principles explaining the behavior of inanimate objects. These concepts were then applied uncritically to the behavior of human beings in the economy. If the creator does not intervene in the affairs of the universe, early laissez faire-oriented economists argued, no possible justification for government interference in the affairs of the market can be offered. An air of absolute truth, therefore, blessed market outcomes and became an accepted ideological position of mainstream economics. Evolutionary economics challenges this alleged divine link:

> Institutionalism denies the existence of absolute truth. This is evidenced . . . in its denial of the existence of natural laws of motion tending us toward an ideal state embodying both truth and merit. . . . (Its) goal is rather the less ambitious one of

> comprehension of the actual workings of the mundane system we inhabit, and the problems it produces, discoverable only through observation of the system itself. In furtherance of this goal, institutionalists seek and incorporate the insights of a wide variety of disciplines. Institutionalism could hardly fail to be interdisciplinary, for it does not define its task simply as a study of markets. . . . Essentially, institutionalists set themselves the task of seeking understanding, rather than truth.
>
> It is a fundamental aspect of institutionalism that the role of economics is to make of this world a better place. . . . In part, this is to be achieved through the avoidance of what to institutional economists seems the highest form of waste—the waste of human potential and fulfillment....The consequences that (institutionalism) seeks are those of a broad public interest.[7]

Therefore, a model built on questionable assumptions is of limited relevance in describing the inter-workings of the economy. Impeccable logic, along with graphical and even mathematical elegance, will still provide faulty results because of those assumptions. The ultimate test of a theory, according to evolutionary economists and others, is empirical verification or observing the theory at work in reality. Empirical observations of pure competition have not been impressive, if they exist at all.

Income Distribution and the Value-Neutral Claim

Many mainstream economists have argued that the output level consistent with long-run equilibrium in pure competition produces a distribution of income and wealth that is both equitable and appropriate. In other words, the existing mix of rich and poor is just as it should be as long as this equilibrium condition is attained. One need not worry that this is the case because mainstream economics depicts the economy as tending toward a position of long run equilibrium. Thus, perfectly competitive markets under the control of those in private business will bring socially desirable results and mainstream theory predicts, even guarantees, this will occur. Not only are these propositions logically dubious but no one has ever offered any proof of their accuracy. Empirical observations of these propositions, therefore, do not exist.

What perhaps bothers evolutionary economists most is the neoclassical claim that the purely competitive model is value free (positive rather than normative) and does not espouse any particular political agenda. With no empirical proof of its validity, the model is used by mainstream economists to justify limited government intervention (laissez faire), an existing distribution of income and wealth that is alleged to be equitable, a belief that control of the economy by those in business will bring maximum benefits to all, and an especially naïve claim that no one can exert undue power and/or influence to use the system to his/her own advantage. Evolutionary economists *reject* all of these claims. Instead, they argue that mainstream economics is *not* value free and has a thinly disguised and easily recognizable political agenda.

The general public, academic specialists in fields other than economics, and institutional economists believe the performance of the economy should be evaluated by some criterion other than whether something called equilibrium is reached. Criteria such as internationally competitive education, effective health care, sufficient job opportunities, efficient production of goods that consumers need, national security, safe neighborhoods, and a clean environment are among those frequently mentioned by these groups as worthwhile. *Long-run equilibrium in pure competition has absolutely nothing to do with the attainment of any of these goals.*

Mainstream obsession with equilibrium is justified by one of the leading advanced microeconomics texts in the following way: "This focus on equilibrium analysis is not due to the belief that equilibrium is necessarily more important than disequilibrium, but rather that the analysis of behavior in disequilibrium is substantially more difficult."[8] In pursuit of a realistic picture, evolutionary economists believe that, difficult though it indeed may be, "analysis of behavior" by a method other than equilibrium must be attempted.

Evolutionary economists study the institution of the small business, seeking ways in which it differs from the large corporation. They also emphasize case studies of specific industries to learn from their changing experiences over time. Although often presented by the mainstream as examples that approximate pure competition, studies of the fishing industry,[9] the potato industry,[10] wholesale nurseries,[11] and even street vendors[12] are clearly within the realm of evolutionary economic research.

In the first three of these, technological advance and resistance to change would be at the forefront of evolutionary analysis. Many aspects of modern agriculture could similarly be studied using this institutional framework. Specific differences in place and time, such as experiences in the United States versus those in developing nations, are also worthy of analysis. The result would be a better understanding of these and other small businesses today, how they have evolved over time, and what some of the problems are that they are likely to face in the unknown and unpredictable future.

Veblenian Technical Efficiency

One other key difference between the mainstream and evolutionary approaches is worth mentioning. Veblen himself developed a concept of technical efficiency but it was different from that offered by mainstream economists.[13] While the neoclassical view is that technical efficiency occurs where P = AC, Veblen proposed an engineering definition that was not cost-based at all. His view was that efficiency resulted when mechanical production processes, using the most advanced technology in existence, manufactured the maximum amount of output possible without waste or idleness. Such a concept focused less on dollars and more on productive work.

Frederic W. Taylor, the mechanical engineer who pioneered "time and motion studies" to improve efficiency in factories, is often considered to be the father of modern management. Following his lead, many engineers in Veblen's day advocated increasing output rather than lowering costs, especially labor costs, as a goal of efficiency. Cost-reduction strategies, however, eventually became the preferred approach of both neoclassical economists and many business managers.

Veblen, Taylor, and many early twentieth-century industrial engineers believed that higher wages, including incentive wages, made labor more productive and stimulated increased output. This is consistent with the view held by contemporary institutionalists that efficiency be defined as workability in terms of solving problems or the enhancement of "individual capabilities and performance."[14] One can only imagine the different direction economics might have taken had one of its cornerstone concepts, efficiency, been defined by the followers of Veblen rather than those of Marshall.

Storytelling and Evolutionary Economics

In an economy dominated by giant corporations, even some mainstream economists are willing to identify the competitive ideal as an analytically useful artificial construct that in practice is at best a rarity. Especially in agriculture, where production methods are becoming more scientific and large agricorporations are emerging, many contend that the perfectly competitive label applied more in some distant past than it does today. Examples of contemporary industries such as fishing, potatoes, wholesale nurseries, and outdoor street markets, however, are still believed by many mainstreamers to possess characteristics that (more or less) fit nearly all the criteria of pure competition. The principles under which these and other industries operate are alleged in textbooks to provide evidence that something close to ideal competition can still be found and may even be somewhat beneficial to consumers. The limited number of potential illustrations and the need to bend the truth slightly here and there, however, remind readers that the fine (or maybe even not so fine) line between ideal and real is still a valid distinction.

Evolutionary economists appreciate both the ingenuity and perseverance of those mainstream economists who still stubbornly seek actual examples of pure competition in practice. The four industries mentioned above, for example, demonstrate some aspects of firm conduct along lines vaguely suggested by their purely competitive model. As long as concepts are stretched somewhat, square pegs may indeed fit into round holes. For example, nurseries, even at the wholesale level, are providing a more diversified selection of plants and gardening aides than ever before. Street markets have always offered more differentiated than standardized products. This is true of both used household items and crafts which incorporate much individual design and creativity. If these non-standardized products can somehow be made into standardized products (by assumption, blind faith, or maybe wishing it were so), then the argument that these are examples of pure competition may be more acceptable, at least to some people.

Perhaps more importantly, such street fairs and farmers' markets flourish primarily because of institutional arrangements that enable their existence. Local government cooperation with community associations often guarantees such steps as no effort to collect sales taxes and adequate security arrangements. Occasional use of community civic centers constitutes an additional institutional set-up that both holds down costs and places an official stamp of approval on such gatherings. When local government in Chicago acquired sufficient power and support to dismantle the city's Maxwell Street market, it did so, ending a near century old institution. The influence of more powerful business groups in the city was an obviously important factor.

Some people, of course, engage in flea market activity more as a hobby than as a source of livelihood. Others merely seek to dispose of long-accumulated items to recapture some small portion of their original cost. Ease of entry and exit is not disputed but many enter as someone other than genuine market participants or aspiring entrepreneurs. Although there are no conspicuous consumers participating, there is pecuniary emulation, as some buyers seek less-expensive imitations or used versions of high-quality products. Habit and tradition often play key roles in drawing participants to flea markets.

In the fishing industry, the mainstream effort to narrow the product to a standardized species is reminiscent of similar classification efforts in agriculture. Are all beets really alike? And how about lobster? Seafood aficionados and gourmet cooks easily dispute the standardized product allegation. To be successful in the business, entry is becoming increasingly expensive and therefore more difficult as boats and other equipment rise in price. Once again, institutional realities may have more to do with who selects this occupation than market forces. Older fishermen have passed the skills on to their children in a manner not unlike the pattern in traditional societies. Immigrants to the United States frequently remain in this profession if that is what they did in their country of origin. Attraction to the ways of the sea (habitual behavior) is often more of a motivating factor than rational pursuit of self-interest.

Potatoes probably provide the strongest case for pure competition among the examples frequently cited. Despite the diversity of products offered, wholesale nurseries may be an artificially contrived example when individual species of plants are considered. Even in these industries, however, any movement toward a single price is highly questionable. The lack of gravitation toward an equilibrium in all cases discussed here speaks for itself.

Analyzing these cases within the framework of the purely competitive market model provides a grossly incomplete picture. Circular and cumulative causation could tell us much about the assortment of economic and noneconomic factors affecting all of these activities. In the early 21st century potato wars between the U. S. and Canada, [15] for example, much more was at stake than potato prices. Involvement of institutions such as the Canadian Food Inspection Agency and the U.S. government, adjustments in the way of life among farmers on both sides of the border, psychological effects of destroyed crops, and emergency credit options provided by banks all deserve mention and would provide a more complete picture of the problem.

Some Perspective

Institutional economists offer the following as worthwhile goals: reasonableness, serviceability, avoiding waste in human potential, and the efficient production of goods that consumers need. According to Veblen, technical efficiency results when mechanical production processes, using the most advanced technology in existence, manufacture the maximum amount of output possible without waste or idleness. When the fishing, potato, and nursery industries do this, they do their job well, even if they do not attain equilibrium.

Broadly focused case studies such as these are telling a story. Storytelling is a familiar method of conveying information in the institutionalist tradition.[16] What happens to farm families when their crops are affected by weather and disease is a more interesting story than whether all of the characteristics of pure competition are met by potato farmers. So is what happens to street vendors who are dependent on income from sales that have been slack for some time and what happens to those who fish for a living when catches become smaller and fewer.

In at least three of these case studies, the technology versus institutions paradigm is especially relevant. Technological advance has affected commercial fishing, nurseries, and all farmers, including those who grow potatoes. Some firms, for example, now use electronic fishing devices such as depth finders and fish finders to locate potential catches. In addition, fairly scientific methods are now used on fish farms and by government-operated agencies which restock depleted waters. Advances in meteorology enable more timely transmission of weather information to those who fish in oceans and in large lakes. Similarly, much technical advance has occurred in operating nurseries where more scientific irrigation and fertilization methods are becoming widespread.

In both fishing and nurseries, institutional resistance to the adoption of new technologies ultimately hurt some firms who have had a difficult time catching up to their more forward-looking rivals. Adherence to the old way of doing things has been a perennial barrier to progress in some farming communities that grow potatoes and other crops. Case studies using the technology versus institutions framework offer a more thorough and more insightful analysis of issues, including the human dimension, than those that focus on whether equilibrium has been attained or all the assumptions of the model have been verified.

With all the emphasis the mainstream supposedly places on precision, it is quite interesting that one of their major cornerstone concepts is so poorly/unrealistically defined and so numerically imprecise. What is even more interesting is the nearly complete absence of mainstream empirical research on the model of pure competition despite its stature as a cornerstone concept in their microeconomics textbooks at all levels. Mainstream journals clearly are not inundated with work even remotely related to this area. Articles on the topic have been limited to philosophical justifications as to why this fictional construct is still meaningful.[17] It is, of course, difficult to imagine any serious attempt at empirical verification of something that does not exist.

What has emerged, partially in response to measurement attempts of the unmeasurable, is a long overdue questioning of existing quantification in economics. In the words of a leader in this field of research, the critique may be summarized as follows: "…..mathematical economics is unreasonably ineffective. Unreasonable, because the mathematical assumptions are economically unwarranted; ineffective because the mathematical formalizations imply non-constructive and uncomputable structures."[18]

One can only hope that this ongoing redefinition within the field of mathematical economics will bury once and for all the countless failed attempts to apply quantification techniques to pure competition, utility, and other mainstream obsessions.

A word of caution is in order. Some (and perhaps much) of this work has formed the basis of methodologies used in the emerging field of behavioral economics. As mentioned in chapter 4 of this book, the field certainly holds much promise. Whether this work ultimately produces realistic insight into the actual behavior of consumers (and business managers facing less than perfect competition) or merely introduces yet more esoteric mathematization remains to be seen.

Footnotes:

1. Joseph E. Pluta, *The Market: Mainstream and Evolutionary Views*, (Dubuque, Iowa: Kendall Hunt Publishing Company, 2008), p. 259.

2. Ki Hoon Kim, "Like Ants to a Picnic," in Ralph T. Byrns and Gerald W. Stone, *Great Ideas for Teaching Economics,* 3rd ed., (Glenview, IL: Scott Foresman and Company), 1987, p. 260.

3. Consumer surplus is the difference between the price a consumer is willing to pay and the price he/she actually pays. It is measured on a graph by the triangular area above the market price and below the demand curve. Producer surplus is the difference between the MC of producing the product and its price. It is measured by the triangular area above the MC curve and below the market price. Under pure competition, both of these areas are supposedly maximized so both consumers and producers are as well off as they possibly

could be.

4. Ramesh Chandra, "Adam Smith and Competitive Equilibrium," *Evolutionary and Institutional Economics Review,* 1, 1, (2004), pp. 57–83. It has also been argued that there are many worthwhile evolutionary elements in the work of Marshall. These, however, have been undermined by his reliance on Herbert Spencer's theoretically flawed evolutionary Social Darwinism. See Geoffrey Hodgson, "Come Back Marshall, All is Forgiven? Complexity, Evolution, Mathematics and Marshallian Exceptionalism", *European Journal of the History of Economic Thought*, 20, 6 (2013), pp. 957-981.

5. Edythe S. Miller, "Economics in a Public Interest: Remarks upon Receiving the Veblen-Commons Award," *Journal of Economic Issues,* 36, 2 (June 2002), pp. 255–256.

6. Miller, pp. 256–257.

7. Miller, pp. 258–259.

8. Hal R. Varian, *Microeconomic Analysis,* 3rd ed., (New York: W. W. Norton and Co.), 1992, p. 1.

9. Background material on competitive elements in the fishing industry may be found in: Frank Asche, Atle Oglend, and Sigbjorn Tveteras, "Regime Shifts in the Fish Meal/Soybean Meal Price Ratio", *Journal of Agricultural Economics*, 64, 1 (February 2013), pp. 97-111; Lee G. Anderson (ed.), *Fisheries Economics: Collected Essays, (*Burlington, VT: Ashgate Publishing, 2002); Dominique M. Duval-Diop and John R. Grimes, "Tales from Two Deltas: Catfish Filets, High Value Foods, and Globalization," *Economic Geography,* 81, 2 *(*April 2005), pp. 177-200; Adrian Saville, "A Comment on the

Management of South Africa's Commercial Fishing Industry," *South African Journal of Economic History,* 16, 1-2 (September 2001), pp. 172-188; and David Shook, "On that Farm He Had Some Fish," *BusinessWeek Online,* August 9, 2001 (http://www.businessweek.com/bwdaily/dnflash/).

10. Information on the potato industry may be found in various issues of *Spudman Magazine* (2000–2015). Other relevant sources for recent developments in agriculture include: Catherine Larochelle and Jeffrey Alwang, "The Role of Risk Mitigation in Production Efficiency: A Case Study of Potato Cultivation in the Bolivian Andes", *Journal of Agricultural Economics*, 64, 2 (June 2013), pp. 363-381; Donatella Baiardi, Carluccio Bianchi, and Eleonora Lorenzini, "Food Competition in World Markets: Some Evidence from a Panel Data Analysis of Top Exporting Countries", *Journal of Agricultural Economics*, 66, 2 (June 2015), pp. 358-391; Catherine Paul et al., "Scale Economies and Efficiency in U.S. Agriculture: Are Traditional Farms History?" *Journal of Productivity Analysis,* 22, 3 (November 2004), pp. 185-205; Douglas Harper, *Changing Works: Visions of a Lost Agriculture,* (Chicago: University of Chicago Press, 2001); and William P. Browne, *The Failure of National Rural Policy,* (Washington, DC: Georgetown University Press), 2001.

11. "Theoretically", a *wholesale* nursery might specialize and grow a single type of standardized product. Perhaps cedar trees or Colorado blue spruce trees or red rose bushes or sego palms or sunflowers or poinsettias? (*Retail* nurseries normally sell a wide diversity of plants, shrubs, and trees so do not qualify.) Instructors who have taught microeconomic principles for a long enough period of time may develop some level of skill in inventing products that can be used as examples of pure competition. In this case, it helps to have

some knowledge of vegetation.

12. A thorough account of street vendor activity may be found at Openair-Market Net, http://www.openair.org/opair/faq.html (retrieved December 2, 2006).

13. Janet T. Knoedler, "Veblen and Technical Efficiency," *Journal of Economic Issues,* 31, 4 (December 1997), pp. 1011–1026.

14. Philip A. Klein and Edythe S. Miller, "Concepts of Value, Efficiency, and Democracy in Institutional Economics," *Journal of Economic Issues,* 30, 1 (March 1996), p. 276.

15. The major issue among normally the friendliest of neighbors was charges of a virus and/or fungus in potatoes grown in the other nation's soil. Both national governments announced restrictions on imports, scientists in each country denounced claims made by rival agriculture representatives, and prices temporarily rose on both sides of the border. Predictably, the conflict was settled without a single shot being fired.

16. Charles K. Wilber and Robert S. Harrison, "The Methodological Basis of Institutional Economics: Pattern Model, Storytelling, and Holism," *Journal of Economic Issues,* 12, 1 (March 1978), pp. 61–90.

17. Louis Makowski and Joseph M. Ostroy, "Perfect Competition and the Creativity of the Market", *Journal of Economic Literature*, 39, 2 (June 2001), pp. 479-535; William Novshek and Hugo Sonnenschein, "General Equilibrium With Free Entry: A Synthetic Approach to the Theory of Perfect Competition", *Journal of Economic Literature*, 25, 3 (September 1987), pp. 1281-1306; P. J. McNulty, "A Note on

the History of Perfect Competition", *Journal of Political Economy*, 75, 4 (August 1967), pp. 395-399; and George J. Stigler, "Pure Competition, Historically Contemplated", *Journal of Political Economy*, 65, 1 (February 1957), pp. 1-17.

18. K. Vela Velupillai, "The Unreasonable Ineffectiveness of Mathematics in Economics", *Cambridge Journal of Economics*, 29, 6 (November 2005), pp. 849-872. See also K. Vela Velupillai, "Uncomputability and Undecidability in Economic Theory", *Applied Mathematics and Computation*, 215, 4 (October 2009), pp. 1404-1416 and K. Vela Velupillai, "Variations on the Theme of Conning in Mathematical Economics", *Journal of Economic Surveys*, 21, 3 (July 2007), pp. 466-505.

Chapter Seven

Deregulation vs. Doing Whatever Works

We don't have a monopoly. Anyone who wants to dig a well without a Hughes bit can always use a pick and shovel.

Howard Hughes

Deregulation has been, above all else, a means of reducing corporate business's accountability to the public.

Herbert Schiller

Conservatives are not necessarily stupid but most stupid people are conservatives.

John Stuart Mill

When your cable TV bill arrives and it is much higher than last month's charges, there is little or nothing that you as a consumer can do. Since there is often only one local provider of cable services and rarely more than two, your only option, after getting angry, might be to purchase your own satellite dish. In the cases of electricity and natural gas, second options may be limited to candles and fireplaces, respectively. If you feel overcharged by your local water company, your only alternative is to drill your own well. When you attend a concert, athletic event, or movie, the prices you pay for drinks and food at concession stands are much higher than those at nearby stores. However, at a football stadium, for example, you are part of a captive audience and buying drinks at grocery store prices is not an option.

When your business must ship bulky items like iron or copper ore from the mine you own to the nearest seaport, the only feasible transportation choice may be the local railroad. Its conveniently located tracks give it a natural advantage over any potential rival, including trucks or ships. If the railroad suddenly raises its prices, you are as powerless as if you were staring into the headlight of a speeding locomotive.

All of these cases are examples of *monopoly,* which has long been an object of suspicion and disrespect in the United States and elsewhere. Aside from being a market structure that is synonymous with the absence of competition, what is it about monopoly that has provoked unrestrained contempt from such sources as Adam Smith himself, numerous works of classical American literature, Hollywood masterpieces including 1946-movie-of-the-year *It's a Wonderful Life,* and popular opinion? Although they have met with mixed success, federal courts and state regulatory commissions have taken dead aim at blatant monopoly practices. While their views, especially with regard to regulation, still vary, neither mainstream economics nor the evolutionary dissent are especially fond of monopoly.

Mainstream View of Monopoly Firms

Condemned by such "authoritative" sources as the Bible and ancient Greek philosophers, monopoly has rarely been viewed favorably. Mainstream economists have primarily used the tools they have developed to explain why monopoly falls far short of ideal competition in terms of efficiency and other criteria.[1] Neither allocative nor technical efficiency is present, barriers to entry prevent competition, and restriction of output allows firms to charge higher prices than those which would prevail if competition were present. Withholding supply transfers some consumer surplus into producer surplus which means that money is taken out of the pockets of consumers and placed in the hands of monopoly firms. It also causes a deadweight loss representing the amount of goods and services which never get produced. Such loss of output and jobs creates reverberations throughout the economy.

Most mainstream economists even acknowledge that monopolies adversely affect the distribution of income and that price discrimination is motivated by a further attempt to capture a significant portion of consumer surplus. Charging different prices to different groups of consumers for essentially the same product is widely practiced by firms with monopoly power including public utilities. Second degree price discrimination or block rate pricing (where utilities charge lower rates to those who use more energy) has negative effects on both the environment and the conservation of resources.

Many monopolies are poorly managed, many of its workers lack motivation, many of its jobs are given to inept relatives and cronies, and many of its decision makers possess more lethargy than energy. As a result, some monopolies experience what mainstream economists call *x-inefficiency*, or actual costs of production that are greater than minimum possible costs due to organizational slack. Any point on the ATC curve represents the lowest possible unit cost of producing that output level. Firms are much more likely to get there if they face cost competition from other firms. Facing no competition, the monopoly might be less cost conscious or more lazy about cost control. In other words, the monopoly may not be on the cost curve at all but somewhere above it. The presence of economies of scale does not necessarily mean that all monopolies are sufficiently motivated to take advantage of them. Many economists believe that, even with economies of scale, monopoly still has higher unit costs than competitive firms because of x-inefficiency.

The Evolutionary View

While the mainstream analysis of monopoly clearly is not complimentary, its primary critique is based on the inability of single firm industries to achieve the efficiency standards of the fictional competitive ideal. The mainstream and evolutionary approaches differ substantially on the issue of what should be done to alleviate the most egregious forms of monopoly excess.

Veblen argued that large firms were more interested in making money than in making goods. Even mainstream graphical analysis suggests that he was correct. Smaller competitive firms produce a relatively large quantity of goods at relatively low prices. Monopolies (and, by inference, large firms that face limited competition) maximize profit at a smaller output level. By focusing on maximum profit (making money), large firms restrict output (do not make some goods) and therefore produce less than would be produced under more competitive conditions, a classic case of *industrial sabotage*.

Veblen further claimed that the instinct of workmanship declines and the craft of salesmanship rises when making money takes precedence over making goods. Production activities slow and increased effort is put into selling what has already been produced. The instinct of workmanship is the pride one takes in one's work, along with the desire to produce high-quality products efficiently. Emphasis on distinctive quality becomes less necessary when a firm is producing for a relatively large market and faces little or no competition. In addition, efficiency is reduced because a large firm is reluctant to introduce new technology until it gets maximum use out of its existing machinery.

This last point logically leads to the much debated question of whether technological innovation and new product development is more likely in monopolies (or other large firms) or smaller more competitive businesses. The most commonly given answer is that competitive firms have the incentive but lack the resources; monopoly firms have the resources but often lack the incentive. Competitive firms need to be efficient and use the most up-to-date *existing* technology. The research and technical advance, however, generally takes place in industries that are nowhere near purely competitive. Lacking economic profits in the long run, few competitive firms are sufficiently endowed with funds needed to experiment with new methods.

Many monopolies, by contrast, receive long-run economic profits. The financial wherewithal for research and development, therefore, is often there. But is the desire? Some mainstream economists argue that, if the opportunity for greater profit exists, (even monopoly) entrepreneurs will respond. If patents and secret processes are an important barrier to entry, the argument continues, why would managers of monopoly firms not seek to increase these entry barriers and thereby enhance their monopoly position?

The problem is that the *lazy monopoly syndrome* in one area often spills over into another. Complacency in holding down costs easily extends into research and development. If competition leads to efficiency, lack of competition likely breeds the reverse. Why seek change when the status quo has been so comfortable? Why invent new technology when existing equipment would have to be replaced before it becomes obsolete? And even if a monopoly reluctantly innovates and eventually reduces its costs, what incentive does it have to translate these cost savings into lower prices to consumers? Padded profit levels are the more likely outcome.

Pursuit of maximum profit is seen in mainstream economics as the driving force behind economic growth. To Veblen and the institutionalists, however, when monopolies (and giant corporations) maximize profit, they produce less than could be produced if more competition existed. In this way, the large firm becomes an institutional restraint on economic progress and pockets profits that could have been used to produce more and meet more consumer needs.

During the final decades of the nineteenth century, the prosperity of giant firms enabled the captains of industry to eliminate smaller competitors and to secure government policies that favored corporate interests. Eventually, public sentiment grew increasingly skeptical about this shameless exercise of raw power. Because of new inventions like electricity and the telephone, the public utilities that provided these services became vital to the operation of businesses and to the lifestyles of consumers. Since substantial economies of scale were present, these utilities were justified as natural monopolies on grounds that one large firm could produce at substantially lower unit cost than several smaller ventures. Continued abuse of monopoly power, however, prompted calls for reform from both consumers and many small business owners.

John R. Commons: Early Institutionalist Influence

Specific government strategies for regulating public utilities were influenced heavily by a number of institutional economists, especially John R. Commons (1862–1945). Together, these reformers provided ideas and helped to draft legislation not only in the areas of regulation but also unemployment compensation, factory safety laws, child labor, and eventually social security. For nearly 30 years, Commons was a leading figure at the University of Wisconsin whose economics department became known as the *Wisconsin school of institutionalism.*[2] His brand of economics was oriented toward political activism. He, along with state Governor Robert La Follette, a Republican who advocated regulation of railroads, played a major role in introducing social reform legislation that became part of the Progressive Era movement between 1900 and 1917.[3] Many of Commons's followers also helped design portions of the New Deal during the 1930s. Indeed, these were the first instances in U.S. history where economists strongly influenced government policy at both the federal and state level. The University of Wisconsin remained heavily oriented toward institutionalism until the 1980s when the dominance of mainstream economics was reestablished there.

Commons believed that institutional economics should be directed toward solving practical problems. He helped to educate an entire generation of economists who were more interested in this approach than in technical mathematical refinements to mainstream economic theory. He believed that the essential elements of the market system should be retained but that abuses in the unregulated free enterprise economy must be prevented. Like Veblen, Commons was not sure that government was always capable of implementing the necessary corrective action but both men opted for experimentation over doing nothing and going forward with whatever worked.

In the view of Commons, regulation promotes entrepreneurship by setting legal boundaries. By policing and penalizing illegal behavior, regulation allows those who operate within the law to be successful without the disadvantage of having to compete with cheaters. Mainstream economists view regulation as an interference with or encroachment upon private rights. Institutional economists view regulation as a means of limiting the power of the town bully.

The type of institutionalism that Commons advocated consisted of a combination of economics, law, and ethics. Legal institutions clearly influence economic behavior. Not only are such legal principles as property rights important, but the courts themselves are constantly providing guidance in the conduct of economic affairs. Changes in the law over time are a prime example of a changing institutional setting in which firms can operate. Evolutionary economists believe careful study of that institutional setting is warranted in order to understand more fully the actual operation of public utilities. Commons saw the legal profession as addressing and seeking the concept of reasonableness. To quote one writer:

> Public utility regulation was concerned with reasonable value, labor law with reasonable wage, workmen's compensation with reasonable safety, and public officials and private citizens were expected to live up to the requirement of reasonable conduct. Commons found little in the writings of the economists that would shed light on the nature of reasonableness.[4]

To Commons, many of the actions of large corporations were anything but reasonable. When public utilities that are monopolies restrict output and charge a higher price for it than would be the case under more competitive conditions, he believed some type of corrective action is necessary to protect those who are powerless to defend themselves. When such firms engage in financial manipulations that benefit selected stockholders and managers but the quality of the product delivered is suspect, he believed prevention of such behavior is required.

Mainstream economic theory with its devotion to nonintervention offered no practical solution to these problems. Therefore, government, despite its limitations, was an obvious source of this corrective action. Procedures for regulating public utilities throughout much of the twentieth century, therefore, were greatly influenced by Commons and other institutional economists. Together, they assisted in creating new regulatory commissions (the first was established in Wisconsin in 1907) and insisted that access to utility products be guaranteed to all buyers.

Mainstream Deregulation

By the 1970s, however, public enthusiasm for regulation declined as energy prices rose, nuclear power plants proved to be expensive, natural gas was in short supply, and American Telephone and Telegraph (AT&T) opposed entry of new firms that offered cost-saving new technologies in telephone service. While managerial ineptness and institutional resistance to change contributed to these problems, consumers and voters were often convinced that regulation was the chief culprit.[5]

During the next two decades, regulatory policies based on principles rooted in institutionalism were increasingly ignored. Whatever approach appeared to encourage competition won favor. Mergers, which had been discouraged by existing federal guidelines, were allowed anyway. Price caps began being used instead of rates based on an allowed return on investment. In this "anything goes" environment, many bankruptcies in public utility–related companies (WorldCom and Enron topped the list) soon followed, along with corporate fraud, plunging stock prices, loan defaults, loss of jobs, depleted employee pension funds, and criminal charges levied against several top executives.

Opponents of regulation continue to be vocal and to influence public policy. Despite widespread abuses by public utilities, not only in recent years but often over the past century, *mainstream criticisms of regulation* have varied little over that time and include the following.

Regulation based on an allowed rate of return provides no incentives to operate efficiently or to pursue technological innovation. Put simply, if a firm is allowed a 10 percent return on its investment, there is no reason for it to hold down its costs. Ten percent of a larger cost figure allows for a larger profit. The inevitable result is an effort to inflate production and operating expenses. Further, regulatory commission obsession with fairness over efficiency results, for example, in higher phone rates charged to businesses, which subsidize residential users, or higher long-distance rates, which subsidize local calling.[6] If profit levels are controlled, the argument continues, there is little reason to introduce new cost-saving machinery that might otherwise raise profits. Of course, the regulatory bureaucracy is judged to be oversized, inefficient, and wasteful.

To mainstream economists, therefore, regulation is not the answer but a major part of the problem itself. Their suggestions for improvement range from deregulation (which has been a disaster, especially in the airline, banking, and energy industries) to a refocusing on price caps and creation of incentives. The latter two may initially sound reasonable based on standards of competitive efficiency.

Evolutionary Evaluation of Deregulation

In most cases, however, evolutionary economists maintain that price caps are set high enough so that substantial economic profits can still be received. The amount of inflation and increases in worker productivity supposedly help to determine price cap levels. Use of both measures, however, is anything but uniform across the nation. For example, since different price index numbers exist, different rates of inflation can be calculated depending on which is used. In practice, incentive regulations are little more than the authority to receive higher rates of return than previously allowed. Specific programs here also vary considerably among the states.

Neither of these readjusted regulatory efforts addresses the question of quality of service. These "reforms" have also resulted in predatory pricing, to the direct detriment of the consumer. There is much evidence in past years that telecommunication companies have inaccurately estimated demand for caller ID, call trace, and other special services.[7] These misestimates have allowed firms to charge higher amounts for these services than their costs justify.

Telephone companies have aggressively sought to diversify their business interests into such fields as cable TV, cell phones, electronic yellow pages, data transmission, financial services, and even real estate. They have been especially active in acquisition of overseas companies across the globe. Diversification into new areas, however, has been shown in many cases not to result in improved efficiency. Managerial efforts to move into high growth potential industries in which they have little or no expertise do more to increase managerial prestige than stock values. In such cases, managers have pursued risky ventures that benefit themselves more than the owners of utility companies.

A firm that produces a wide variety of products is capable of shifting its costs among them in ways that add to its profit and thus benefit the firm while harming others. When firms generate multiple products and production of some is regulated while production of others is not, it is common for those firms to arbitrarily assign costs to their regulated output. This allows them to charge a higher regulated price than would otherwise be justified. It also enables them to show higher profits in their unregulated segment of production. In effect, they are cross-subsidizing their unregulated activity to the detriment of their competitors in that area, while artificially inflating prices in their regulated activity to the detriment of consumers in that area.

In other words, firms with the market power to define and rearrange their cost structures will likely do so in ways that benefit themselves at the expense of those who lack such power. When the multiple plants in question are located in different states and even different countries, the jurisdiction of regulatory commissions may not be clearly defined. As a result, their ability to do their job in the interest of consumers may be jeopardized.

Harry M. Trebing, arguably the leading public utility economist during the latter half of the twentieth century, has suggested that, as management has become more interested in new technologically advanced operations, basic telephone service has deteriorated both in wireline and wireless services as well as in both long distance and local service.[8]

Evolutionary economists today advocate government intervention that sets high performance standards and forces public utilities to pay penalties whenever those standards are not met. They also endorse close monitoring of potential fraud. They further challenge the claim made by mainstream economists that deregulation has produced lower prices for consumers of electricity, natural gas, and telecommunications services. Rather, they argue that while deregulation:

> has led to lower prices for industrial and larger commercial customers, the same is not true for smaller commercial and residential customers. More importantly, if the present template for deregulation continues to be applied, there is the possibility that prices will actually increase while service decreases for residential and most commercial customers.[9]

Evolutionary economists see in deregulation an evolving process whereby large utility firms have become even larger. As this has occurred, they have become more able to practice what Veblen called industrial sabotage, or the conscious withdrawal of efficiency. In other words, they have been able to restrict output and raise prices.

> This is best demonstrated by the behavior of El Paso (Energy Corporation), which has become the world's largest broadly based natural gas company. It owns the nation's largest complex of pipelines.......and two-thirds of its revenues came from nonregulated sources. California charged that it withheld transmission capacity, thereby driving prices in the California market to $23 per mcf versus $7 per mcf across the U.S. market. El Paso reached a settlement with California.......whereby El Paso would pay $1.1 billion in compensation over twenty years.[10]

Evolutionary economists believe that deregulation to achieve competition in industries like electric power is misguided because true competition in this type of industry is impossible. There are two reasons why this is the case. The first is that the product is standardized (electricity per kilowatt hour), not differentiated. The second is that fixed costs (overhead costs) are very high. Some examples illustrate why profits are unlikely under competition when either of these conditions holds.[11]

Agricultural products are the classic example of a (relatively) standardized output produced under highly competitive conditions. When farmers overproduce (have a bumper crop), prices fall dramatically. In an effort to stay in business, farmers naturally seek government programs to limit production and/or support prices. Any attempt to collude with each other (even if it were legal) is impossible, given the large number of sellers in the market. Large corporations that produce standardized products (in industries where the number of sellers is much smaller) have sought similar ends by cooperating with each other, either legally or illegally.

History is filled with examples of this type of behavior in such industries as steel, vitamins, and other products. Price fixing and/or output restrictions in all of these industries eventually resulted in federal laws outlawing such actions. The initial efforts, however, were undertaken because competition forced prices and profit levels downward. In search of higher profits, large firms did what they believed they had to do.

Laws reduced but did not eliminate such activity, as some sellers evidently felt the risk was worth taking. Mergers and efforts to differentiate products were inevitably undertaken to limit competition and gain some amount of monopoly power. Fully deregulating energy production, allowing cooperation among sellers, making the antitrust laws more permissive, and allowing mergers to occur without restraint would likely result in a replay of this earlier scenario.

High fixed costs similarly limit profit opportunities under highly competitive conditions. Electric service and other utilities clearly have fixed costs that comprise a large portion of their total costs. Such firms must, therefore, be large in order to take advantage of economies of scale but must still be able to set prices above average total cost in order to receive an economic profit. If many firms exist, they may not be able to produce enough in order to enjoy the benefits of all economies of scale.

The only ways for competing firms producing standardized products with high fixed costs to remain profitable are to collude with each other in order to keep prices high or to practice price discrimination. The first option is illegal under U. S. antitrust law, while the second violates the stated goals of many states and the Federal Energy Regulatory Commission to provide the service at just, reasonable, and nondiscriminatory rates. As a result, evolutionary economists conclude that electric power can be provided only if electric utilities are regulated or government owned.

In the airline industry, supporters of deregulation ignored or refused to acknowledge the extent to which government involvement existed and was inevitable. Because of the important role airlines and aerospace play in national defense and because of the unique character of aviation technology, government has always been heavily active in the industry. Its continued involvement is certain as safety considerations accelerate in an age of terrorism. Using a noninterventionist competitive model as the basis for deregulation makes little sense since the industry never has and never will approximate highly competitive conditions. As one observer has commented:

> In this industry, governments initiate ideas and take them to business. Companies initiate ideas and take them to government. Ideas grow out of the interchange. Governments finance development. Companies finance development. There is joint financing. Product design proceeds with governments and companies interchanging at every stage. Consumption of the service is under comprehensive government supervision. Deregulation changes none of this. Rather the industry remains an inexorable mix of social and private interests that bears little resemblance to neoclassical assumptions.[12]

Conclusion

In the technology versus institutions paradigm, those policies that promote technological advance contribute to economic progress. Recent efforts at deregulation, however, have not led to innovation or to expanding knowledge of public utility production processes. Evidence of this can be seen in the fact that development of green power has only taken place when it has been required by state law. Deregulation in itself has not been a factor in promoting use of wind as an energy source and has actually increased reliance on traditional energy sources and the added pollution they bring.

As mergers occur, a number of diversified services (such as phone and Internet access provided by the same firm) acquire significant monopoly power and move closer to becoming large monopoly firms. Once again, the approach of mainstream economics does not adequately address the issue of power relationships, which it more or less assumes do not exist. Is it possible, perhaps, that the mainstream approach to public utility regulation is itself experiencing diminishing returns?

The original goal of public utility regulation as envisioned by Commons and other early institutionalist writers was to protect the public interest. The new deregulation has ignored, and therefore been harmful to, the public interest and instead has protected large utility companies.[13] Indeed, many contemporary advocates of deregulation discredit the public interest as a naïve and outmoded concept. Rather than maximizing profit, which serves private interests, evolutionary economists favor maximizing productive potential, which serves the public interest, a concept that they still respect.

Footnotes:

1. Consult any mainstream principles or intermediate microeconomics text to verify this statement and the mainstream arguments which follow.

2. His leading works include John R. Commons, *Institutional Economics: Its Place in Political Economy,* (Madison: University of Wisconsin Press, 1934) and John R. Commons, *The Legal Foundations of Capitalism,* (Madison: University of Wisconsin Press, 1924).

3. John Milton Cooper Jr., *Pivotal Decades: The United States, 1900–1920,* (New York: W. W. Norton and Company, 1990), especially pp. 91–92.

4. Henry W. Spiegel, *The Growth of Economic Thought,* (Englewood Cliffs, New Jersey: Prentice Hall, 1971), p. 637.

5. Harry M. Trebing, "Assessing Deregulation: The Clash Between Promise and Reality," *Journal of Economic Issues,* 38, 1 (March 2004), pp. 2–3. See also Osha Gray Davidson, *The Bush Legacy: An Assault on Public Protections*, (Washington, D. C.: Center for Effective Government, 2009).

6. Edythe S. Miller, "Economic Regulation and the Social Contract: An Appraisal of Recent Developments in the Social Control of Telecommunications," *Journal of Economic Issues,* 28, 3 (September 1994), p. 800. For a more recent assessment with similar results, see: *Robert W. Crandall, Competition and Chaos: U. S. Telecommunications Since the 1996 Telecom Act*, (Washington, D. C.: Brookings Institution, December 2004).

7. Miller, p. 809.

8. Trebing, p. 9.

9. Thomas C. Gorak, "Taking the Road Less Traveled: Harry Trebing and the Mythology of Deregulation," in Edythe S. Miller and Warren J. Samuels (eds.), *An Institutionalist*

*Approach to Public Utility Regulation, (*East Lansing, Michigan: Michigan State University Press, 2002), p. 387. For a more up to date confirmation of the points made here, see Eric Nalder, "Deregulation in Texas Fails to Make Power More Reliable, Cheap," *Houston Chronicle,* January 13, 2013.

10. Trebing, p. 12.

11. The argument presented here draws on Eugene P. Coyle, "Public Control, through Ownership or Regulation, Is Necessary in Electric Power," in Miller and Samuels, pp. 362–367. See also Tyson Slocum, *The Failure of Electricity Deregulation: History, Status, and Needed Reforms,* (Washington, D. C.: Public Citizen's Energy Program, 2007).

12. Bill Wilkins, "Airline Deregulation: Neoclassical Theory as Public Policy," *Journal of Economic Issues,* 18, 2 (June 1984), p. 425. See also Amy L. Fraher, *The Next Crash: How Short Term Profit Seeking Trumps Airline Safety*, (Ithaca, NY: Cornell University Press, 2014) and Robert Kuttner, "Airline Deregulation Should Be Scrapped," *The Baltimore Sun*, August 8, 2013.

13. Joseph E. Pluta, "The Failure of Deregulation in the Telecommunications, Energy, and Airline Industries", *Perspectives in Business*, 5, 1 (Spring 2008), pp. 11-18.

Chapter Eight

Veblen, Chamberlin, and the Small Business

About half of what separates the successful entrepreneurs from the non-successful ones is pure perseverance.

Steven Jobs

If you're passionate about something and you work hard, then I think you will be successful.

Pierre Omidyar

By working faithfully eight hours a day, you may eventually get to be boss and work twelve hours a day.

Robert Frost

Millions of Americans dream of owning their own business. Besides the opportunity to unleash their entrepreneurial spirit, many are attracted by the respect that small business owners receive. Most Americans detest monopoly and many often look suspiciously at large corporations even if they are not monopolies. In the eyes of many consumers, such corporate giants in recent years appear increasingly impersonal and, in far too many instances, unethical.

The small business owner, by contrast, is generally viewed as hard-working, independent, and in touch with the needs of consumers. He or she is usually well known in the community and, in turn, knows many customers on a first-name basis. We all have a favorite store or group of stores we patronize because we feel we are treated well there. Each small business strives to provide some unique feature, ranging from its convenient location to the clerk's friendly smile. Such firms are highly competitive, although they clearly do not fit the model of pure competition.

Mainstream Imperfect Competition

Prior to the 1930s, economists primarily studied market behavior in terms of either pure competition or monopoly. Because most industries did not fit neatly into either polar extreme, efforts to explain intermediate market settings were eventually undertaken. Two contributions, each made independently but both published in 1933, form the basis of our current understanding.

Edward Chamberlin of Harvard University called his model *monopolistic competition,* which suggests that it represents a market setting somewhere in between monopoly and pure competition. Joan Robinson[1] of Cambridge University in England called her model *imperfect competition,* apparently to emphasize that it represents a market setting closer to the competitive ideal than monopoly. For all practical purposes, the two terms are interchangeable and are aimed at describing the world of the typical small to medium sized American business. Such a business environment includes a large number of firms, product differentiation, some control over price, ease of entry and exit, a strong tendency to advertise, some attention to market share, and certain elements of rivalry.

Mainstream graphical analysis of imperfect competition emphasizes the highly elastic demand due to a large number of substitute products available as well as the ease of entry and exit which eventually leads to a long run equilibrium where only normal profits are earned. Excess capacity, price wars, advertising to achieve economies of scale and to lower elasticity, and maximizing total revenue instead of profit in pursuit of market share are also given some attention.

Some Observations

The model does provide a somewhat more realistic framework for analyzing today's highly competitive markets than the model of pure competition. Small to medium sized firms do enter an industry when economic profits exist and leave when losses persist. Many small businesses do operate with excess capacity. This wasted space and slightly higher prices to consumers, however, appear to be a small price to pay for the wide range of offerings that product differentiation brings. No one would want to see widespread standardization of consumer goods in the name of full capacity operation and slightly lower prices.

Product differentiation is clearly more art than science and may be real or imagined. What matters to the seller is that consumers believe that such differences exist. One is reminded of the cartoon in which a woman watching a TV commercial says to her husband: "I never realized until this moment that what we need to make our marriage successful is an electric toothbrush with a built in CD player." Of course, no one needs such an absurd contraption! No doubt one does not even exist. But if enough consumers *believe* what the woman in the cartoon does, the eye of the seller will be opened and the item will be mass produced.

A product that is different, however, does not automatically insure success.[2] In the late 1950s, the Ford Motor Company introduced the Edsel, its "car of the future." It was different, especially in its styling. It was also the most dismal failure in the history of the automobile industry. In 1985, the Coca-Cola Company changed the formula of its long time popular soft drink. The taste of the new version was definitely different. Consumers protested so loudly that the company was forced to bring back the original formula, which it embarrassingly renamed Coca-Cola Classic.

Thousands of new business ideas fail every year. Different is not always better. The consumer is a fickle judge. What matters is not that the product is useful or legitimately better. Rather, it is the perception in the mind of the consumer that the product is better that matters. To that end, advertisers have been trying to manipulate the consumer psyche for at least a century. Chain stores and other large producers have led the charge. Despite the huge advertising budgets of the chains, small family-run businesses have not only survived but thrived. Apparently, American consumers still appreciate the personal touch and a dedication to quality.

An unusually unique seller, such as a hotel owner with a property located in the magnificent Canadian (or even American) Rockies, may earn substantial economic profit even in the long run. More often, however, the large number of firms and free entry force prices to the point where profit margins are low, whether or not they are actually only normal profit.

Among retailers, for example, discount stores performed extremely well and, therefore, earned economic profits during the late 1990s. Especially where stores had been modernized and the range of merchandise had expanded, firms such as Wal-Mart, Kmart, Target, and Dollar General drew a fairly large number of upper-income consumers. Hot items included sporting goods, grills, patio furniture, home electronics, and appliances. As the decade drew to a close, however, discount stores were under huge pressure to cut prices in order to keep customers. Predictably, profit margins fell. Kmart even had to file for bankruptcy but subsequently reorganized and began selling on a smaller scale. Kmart was later acquired by Sears in 2005.

American foreign policy has consistently promoted democracy as the best hope for the survival of the global market system. Despite the potential abuses and waste inherent in mass advertising, the best hope for the survival of domestic markets may well be found in the strength of its vibrant, small, imperfectly competitive businesses. This argument becomes increasingly attractive as corporate scandals multiply and dominate headlines.

Small firms are not immune to criminal behavior. The localized environments in which most operate coupled with fewer layers of managerial bureaucracy, however, make such behavior easier to detect and prosecute. Small firms also allow for market forces to work more effectively. If a local real estate developer, for example, is accused of questionable practices, consumers can easily switch to other developers. Image problems for a relatively small firm in a local area may be difficult to overcome. The network of shady practices involving several co-conspirators in the corporate world, however, may take years to sort out. In the meantime, consumers are uncertain who is worthy of their trust and who is not.

Among smaller firms, one of the biggest deceptions occurs when a chain purchases a family run business and continues to use the family name. Consumers are led to believe they are buying from a firm that has built a reputation on its personal one-on-one business dealings. In reality, such a firm is often owned by an impersonal corporation not especially interested in providing the one-on-one relationships made famous by the name behind which it currently hides.

Despite their imperfections, small businesses are the backbone of the U.S. economy. They create millions of jobs and allow rugged individualists to innovate and deliver numerous goods and services that meet consumer needs. Small business owners are among the most hard-working, intelligent, and creative people on the planet. They also possess a record of integrity and honesty that managers of large business firms can often only envy.

Veblen's Influence on Chamberlin

Many aspects of the theory of imperfect competition appeal to evolutionary economists. There are several reasons why this is true. When originally devised in the 1930s, the theory was presented as a dissent against the model of pure competition. Such dissent, of course, is an essential feature of the evolutionary approach. Edward Chamberlin, one of the authors who advanced the model, was influenced by Veblen and credited him in his landmark book and afterward.

The connection between the two men may have been even closer. Chamberlin's book is actually a revised version of his 1927 doctoral dissertation at Harvard University. Allyn A. Young, a colleague and friend of Veblen when the two were at Stanford University, was Chamberlin's dissertation advisor who supervised the work on monopolistic competition at Harvard.[3] In the 1933 published book, Chamberlin quotes Veblen's 1904 *Theory of Business Enterprise* regarding the pervasiveness of a *monopoly element* in the modern economy. Both men use this term in their critique of the neoclassical purely competitive model.

The similarity in the two books may even be more pronounced since both discuss market power, selling costs, and advertising. All are key concepts in the modern version of the theory. Chamberlin also credits Veblen with inspiring his notion of product differentiation through Veblen's discussion in the *Theory of Business Enterprise* of the customs and prestige associated with goodwill, trademarks, and brands.[4] Similarities between mainstream and evolutionary thinking on product differentiation are well documented.[5]

Like some institutionalists, Chamberlin attempted to build on and modify neoclassical theory rather than dismantle it entirely. He himself considered his theory to be evolutionary; he believed he was describing a process of how markets evolve over time. Selling costs and advertising deal with human habits and customs, factors that institutionalists emphasize.[6] Cultural influences on consumer buying patterns and consumer response to advertising are, therefore, important. This fact was not seriously considered by mainstream economists before Chamberlin.

Chamberlin also explicitly addresses the possibility that equilibrium might not be attained in his model of the small business firm. Most mainstream texts, however, have focused instead on that part of his analysis that (reluctantly?) used the equilibrium concept. The contemporary imperfectly competitive model begins to deviate from the neoclassical assumption that firms maximize profit. By surveying other options such as cost minimization and revenue maximization (maximum market share), the door is being opened to considering alternative possibilities of entrepreneurial and managerial motivations.

Newtonian calculus, which enables one to find maximum and minimum values, will still apply to some of these motives but not to others (i.e., those that set a goal other than maximizing or minimizing something). Such goals as widespread consumer satisfaction and favorable image in the community come to mind. So do more self-serving goals like limiting the amount of unsold inventory and maintaining stable or even friendly relationships with wholesalers.

Unlike the dated purely competitive ideal, the model of imperfect competition deals with contemporary institutions (i.e., small- and medium-sized business firms), some of which may be able to exert a certain degree of market power. Institutionalists see the model of imperfect competition as more holistic than the competitive ideal. In this whole, all aspects of human behavior interact. The broad-based discussion of the many factors giving rise to product differentiation is consistent with the holistic method. So are the many continuous adjustments that are required because the number of product variations is virtually unlimited. Some institutionalists, therefore, consider the model of imperfect competition to complement both their mode of analysis and their way of addressing issues related to the economy. Through Veblen's influence on Chamberlin, evolutionary economists may have influenced mainstream economics far more than they are generally given credit.

Some Practical Institutionalist Research

In studying the institution of the small business, evolutionary economists often provide insight into such areas as the retail business potential of inner cities,[7] government policy toward small business entrepreneurship,[8] the extent to which agricultural goods are becoming differentiated products,[9] and potential competition from manufacturers in Mexico.[10] Other topics being studied include the role of microfinance in entrepreneurship and community building,[11] pricing policies used by wholesalers and retailers,[12] the rising cost of health insurance benefits,[13] the accuracy of *Wall Street Journal* economic forecasts,[14] and ownership of small pharmacies.[15]

Finally, there are groups of evolutionary economists addressing proposals for changes in the software industry,[16] community associations and the housing market,[17] the large number of entrepreneurs among different ethnic minorities,[18] trends in female entrepreneurship globally,[19] and efforts by economists to avert the financial crisis of 2007.[20] All of these case studies provide information to prospective entrepreneurs who seek a dynamic approach that describes how relevant experiences have changed over time.

Many of their critics claim that institutional economists are primarily negative in their dissent from the mainstream and offer no constructive guidance that the general population might seek from professional economists. Some go so far as to assert that Veblen and his followers were hopelessly anti-business. Contrary to this view, the above fourteen recent case studies use evolutionary methods to provide practical and useful information to those who aspire to become entrepreneurs. Additional case studies not cited here add to this valuable literature.

Some mainstream economists use their tools of choice in research of similar value to small business owners. Others, however, whose goal is to establish more rigidly defined and mathematically precise laws, miss the opportunity to offer valuable assistance to a sector of the economy that has been a driving force in job creation and in meeting consumer wishes.

Footnotes:

1. Nahid Aslanbeigui and Guy Oakes, *The Provocative Joan Robinson: The Making of a Cambridge Economist*, (Durham, NC: Duke University Press, 2009).

2. Roger LeRoy Miller, Daniel K. Benjamin, and Douglass C. North, "The Perils of Product Differentiation," in *The Economics of Public Issues,* 19th ed., (Boston: Addison Wesley, 2015).

3. Steven Sawyer, "The Influence of Thorstein Veblen's *Theory of Business Enterprise* on the Economic Theories of Edward Chamberlin," *Journal of Economic Issues,* 38, 2 (June 2004), pp. 553–561.

4. Edward H. Chamberlin, *The Theory of Monopolistic Competition, (*Cambridge, MA: Harvard University Press, 1933), p. 60.

5. William Breit and Kenneth G. Elzinga, "Product Differentiation and Institutionalism: New Shadows on an Old Terrain," *Journal of Economic Issues,* 8, 4 (December 1974),

pp. 813–826.

6. A. D. Peterson, "Chamberlin's Monopolistic Competition: Neoclassical or Institutional?" *Journal of Economic Issues,* 13, 3 (September 1979), pp. 669–686.

7. Stephan Weiler et al., "Understanding the Retail Business Potential of Inner Cities," *Journal of Economic Issues,* 37, 4 (December 2003), pp. 1075–1105.

8. Rachel Parker, "Coordination and Competition in Small Business Policy: A Comparative Analysis of Australia and Denmark," *Journal of Economic Issues,* 36, 4 (December 2002), pp. 935–952.

9. Patricia Aust Stearns and Thomas Reardon, "Determinants and Effects of Institutional Change: A Case Study of Dry Bean Grades and Standards," *Journal of Economic Issues,* 36, 1 (March 2002), pp. 1–16.

10. Janet M. Tanski and Dan W. French, "Capital Concentration and Market Power in Mexico's Manufacturing Industry: Has Trade Liberalization Made a Difference?" *Journal of Economic Issues,* 35, 3 (September 2001), pp. 675–711.

11. Tonia Warnecke, "The 'Individualist Entrepreneur' vs. Socially Sustainable Development: Can Microfinance Build Community?" *Journal of Economic Issues,* 48, 2 (June 2014), pp. 377–386.

12. Robert L. Steiner, "A Dual Stage View of the Consumer Goods Economy," *Journal of Economic Issues,* 35, 1 (March 2001), pp. 27–44.

13. Rudy Fichtenbaum and Paulette Olson, "The Impact of Unionization on Health Insurance Benefits," *Journal of Economic Issues,* 36, 2 (June 2002), pp. 323–330.

14. Mark R. Greer, "Can the *Wall Street Journal*'s Economic Forecasters Predict Turning Points?" *Journal of Economic Issues,* 40, 3 (September 2006), pp. 808–812.

15. Dan Friesner, "Institutional Policy-Making in (In)Action: The Case of Pharmacy Ownership in North Dakota," *Journal of Economic Issues,* 43, 4 (December 2009), pp. 1025-1042.

16. Serhat Kologlugil, "Free Software, Business Capital, and Institutional Change: A Veblenian Analysis of the Software Industry", *Journal of Economic Issues,* 46, 4 (December 2012), pp. 831–858.

17. William H. Rogers, "Planning in the Housing Market and Bellamy's Influence on Private Governments," *Journal of Economic Issues,* 38, 1 (March 2004), pp. 253–266.

18. Gamal Ibrahim and Vaughan Galt, "Ethnic Business Development: Toward a Theoretical Synthesis and Policy Framework," *Journal of Economic Issues,* 37, 4 (December 2003), pp. 1107–1119.

19. Tonia Warnecke, "Entrepreneurship and Gender: An Institutionalist Perspective," *Journal of Economic Issues,* 47, 1 (June 2013), pp. 455–463.

20. Martha A. Starr, "Contributions of Economists to the Housing-Price Bubble," *Journal of Economic Issues,* 46, 1 (March 2012), pp. 143–171.

Chapter Nine

Does "Creative Psychiatry" Help or Mislead Consumers?

Half the money I spend on advertising is wasted; the trouble is, I don't know which half.
John Wanamaker

Advertising is the art of convincing people to spend money they don't have for something they don't need.
Will Rogers

Advertising is legalized lying.
H. G. Wells

No matter where they go, consumers are constantly inundated with sales pitches, catchy jingles, cute slogans, and artificial images. Driving home from work, we pass thirty billboards and listen to ten minutes of music with fifteen minutes of commercials on the radio. Upon arrival, we discard numerous pieces of junk mail, read over a magazine with thirty pages of news articles and fifty pages of ads, and watch television where we are interrupted every ten minutes for a "word from our sponsor." The phone may ring more than once with a message from our friendly telemarketer trying to sell us something we could not imagine wanting. Our personal computer, once a haven from such bombardment, often has unsolicited windows popping up when we are attempting to use the Internet. And somehow, those telemarketers have found a way to get our e-mail address and deliver endless quantities of electronic junk mail, some of which is able to bypass our diligent spam-filtering systems.

Even movie theaters now run a string of ad spots before their audience can see previews and the feature attraction. When we attend a professional athletic event, signs (many of them electronic) are everywhere, the players wear shoes they were paid to wear, an overhead blimp reappears periodically, and the program we purchased has more ads than information about the teams. Perhaps the ultimate insult is having to listen to an ad on a speaker as we pump expensive gasoline into our car tanks. It is almost as if we must endure the propaganda of an oil company as they rob us.

Are we better off because of all the ads we see and hear? Or has the typical consumer reached the point of diminishing returns long ago? These questions are controversial and their answers depend on your perspective. A summary of some of the leading arguments follows. The strategies of modern advertising clearly give new meaning to an industry that Veblen described as "creative psychiatry" and whose executives he sarcastically christened "publicity engineers".

Some Potentially Beneficial Effects

There are those who believe that advertising encourages product differentiation, which in turn satisfies a wide range of consumer wishes and may even prompt entry of new firms.[1] The optimistic tone of this contention suggests that everyone is made better off when ads proliferate. Ads clearly do enable firms to make their differentiation claims to a wide audience, if in fact that is the message their ads emphasize.

Advertising promotes brand recognition,[2] which places an identifiable standard in the minds of consumers. When traveling somewhere you have never been before, staying at a Ramada Inn or eating at a Pizza Hut assures a known experience. The local Cozy Motel or family-run Patty's Pizza Pie Place might be higher quality but might also be worse. The traveler would be wise to solicit some guidance from local residents or from travel guides available in bookstores and online. Many tourists, however, do not take the time to do this and feel more comfortable minimizing the number of surprises by going with a firm that has a proven track record, even if its quality is not top of the line.

Some consumers no doubt assume that if a smaller firm can afford advertising, it must be reputable or at least more established than other lesser known, potentially fly-by-night operations. This may especially be the case involving services for which a consumer may have only an occasional need. Tuxedo rental, flowers for special events, plumbing needs, and funeral homes are cases in point. Attractive Web sites or large ads in the old yellow pages of the phone book (remember?) certainly catch a consumer's eye more than a mere listing. Such messages convey a certain amount of experience which may be a valuable factor in consumer choice.

Advertising enables the media to offer their products at lower costs than would otherwise be the case. Newspapers, magazines, and Internet service would be far more expensive if advertisers did not buy ads. Network television is "free" to viewers, the argument continues, because advertisers pay most of their bills. As a result, the public is inexpensively entertained and may learn something about various products as well.

Successful advertising *may* result in lower prices for the consumer.[3] If advertising raises demand, firms produce more and unit costs fall. This result occurs if economies of scale are present because average cost falls as output rises. Even though total costs are higher, those costs may be spread over a larger number of consumers so that unit costs may be significantly less.

In theory, advertising is supposed to help consumers make rational decisions and decrease the cost of learning about products.[4] This argument is valid when advertising is genuinely informative. When an ad gives an accurate description of product quality and its price, when it makes information available on new products or product improvements, or when it emphasizes some unique aspect of a product, advertising can help consumers in making choices.

Some examples include new whitening agents in Ajax cleanser, scientific tests that document people who brushed with Crest toothpaste experienced fewer cavities, or improved technology in products ranging from smart phones to razors. Particularly useful features may be found in comparative ads, which quantify such things as the strength of pain relievers like Bayer, Excedrin, Advil, and Aleve; the nutritional content of various fruit juices; or even the number of calories in light beers like Michelob Light, Miller Lite, and Pearl Light.[5]

Besides pushing its product, advertising may provide socially useful encouragement in areas such as health care.[6] Breakfast cereal ads may have made nutrition-minded consumers more aware of specific vitamins and minerals. Toothpaste ads may raise awareness of the benefits of regular dental care.[7] Ads for exercise equipment may demonstrate the advantages of a healthy lifestyle. Public service messages that discourage drug and alcohol abuse, encourage teenagers to stay in school, tell people not to litter, or laud the efforts of charitable organizations such as the United Way certainly provide positive advice. Such ads may be especially powerful if their message is delivered by a well-known athlete, rock star, or movie celebrity.[8]

Some Potentially Misleading Effects

Although many television ads are entertaining, their informational content is often zero. Regrettably, some ads contain more misinformation and questionable claims than facts. Several magazine ads in the 1920s actually stated that cigarette smoking was soothing for the throat. Listerine at that time was sold not only as a prevention against bad breath but also as a cure for dandruff, baldness, and excessive underarm perspiration. Other ads in the 1930s and 1940s showed African American dishwashers and maids speaking in stereotypical uneducated black dialect.[9] What "information" was presented here?

These extremely exploitive and medically false claims have disappeared, in part because of government oversight of the industry. Inaccuracies today are more subtle but equally disturbing. The inference that a brand-name athletic shoe or breakfast cereal enables an NBA player to soar above opposing team members is laughable. The young, physically fit male and female bodies shown in beer commercials are unlikely to stay that way for long if they continue to consume the product the ads endorse. These and other similar pitches apparently strive more for name recognition in the mind of the consumer than for assistance in making rational choices. The Federal Trade Commission has the legal authority to prevent false and misleading advertising. Despite their vigilance, only the most blatant abuses have been targeted and clever advertising executives often successfully sidestep federal challenges.

There are high social costs involved in advertising.[10] Some city streets are so littered with huge signs that it may be harder, not easier, for the motorist to find what he or she is seeking. Flashing electronic signs at professional football games make it more difficult to watch the players a fan paid to see. Billboards detract from the beauty of the countryside.

The argument is even more compelling when one considers the potential influence advertisers exert on the communications media. Suppose, for example, that there is a lawsuit filed against a major corporation and that the firm is at fault. Will a leading news magazine give an unbiased report if the corporation advertises heavily in that publication? Will a newspaper in a small town dominated by racists give an accurate account of the benefits of ethnic and cultural diversity?

Advertisers sometimes pull their ads if they do not like the theme of a television show. Such actions occurred to protest the Ellen DeGeneres "promotion" of the lesbian lifestyle and the Disney Corporation's provision of health benefits to its employees who are gay couples. Many Americans are quite uncomfortable with the ability advertisers have to dictate social mores and even influence the accuracy of news reports. Corporate support of Fox News guarantees that large business firms and the politicians who support them are portrayed positively, and not always truthfully, whenever they are involved in controversy.

Despite some claims to the contrary, the free TV and cheap newspaper/magazine argument is invalid.[11] The consumer pays for TV indirectly when buying the product advertised. In addition, when advertisers pay for TV, they merely redistribute the cost of television to many people who do not even watch it but do use the products advertised. When a soft drink or beer manufacturer pays $1.5 million for a thirty-second spot during the Super Bowl, someone must pay that bill. As long as the firms are profitable and still in business, that someone is the consumer. So enjoy that professionally produced entertaining TV ad as you sip your beverage of choice. If it is the same beverage being advertised, you paid for the ad when you bought that six pack.

Advertising may lower a firm's average costs but not necessarily prices to the consumer. Suppose advertising by a firm achieves the desired result of realizing economies of scale and lowering the firm's unit costs. Not all businesses, however, will lower their prices. Because of ease of entry in industries composed of a large number of highly competitive small businesses, a new firm may advertise to stimulate demand and experience economies of scale. When existing firms face this new competition, they cut prices and consumers benefit. In an industry where there are only a few large firms, however, both new entry and price competition are less likely.[12] As a result, the benefits of cost cuts may not be passed along in the form of lower prices.

Sometimes, advertising is ineffective. When it does not result in an increase in sales, it simply has not worked. A recent study, for example, has documented that a 400 percent increase in advertising expenditures over the span of four decades had virtually no direct effect on sales of alcoholic beverages.[13] Who paid for these ads? Obviously, consumers of the product. (Jobs provided to advertising executives and entertainment provided by TV commercials are rather weak justifications for this activity.) This waste of resources is one of the strongest arguments against advertising. People paid to produce these ads produced nothing and achieved nothing.

Further, advertising may benefit an individual firm but not the economy as a whole. If advertising by one firm takes customers away from another, the first firm's average costs may fall but the second firm's average costs will rise. A substantial part of the money spent on advertising does not lead to economies of scale at all. Much advertising is simply retaliatory; it counterpunches the ad of a competing firm. Such efforts primarily add to prices paid by consumers.

The argument that advertising assists in making rational choices has been challenged frequently. This is particularly true when ads contain little or no information, make ridiculous claims, or include endorsements from famous people who obviously appear because they are well paid to do so, not because they genuinely know or even believe this item is superior. When consumers respond to such ads, how rational can they possibly be?

Not all ads encourage beneficial behavior. While some may have improved health awareness, others have shamelessly encouraged harmful habits. Until the ban on cigarette advertising on TV, tobacco companies sold cancer along with their cigarettes.[14] Violent computer games have long been suspected of planting the seeds of criminal behavior in young people. One study of ads in twenty-seven gun magazines found that firearms generally were presented as part of a lifestyle, self-protection was mentioned infrequently, and attributes of the gun (especially technological characteristics) were noted in almost every ad.[15]

Sexual stereotypes have diminished in recent years but women are still often portrayed in traditional and subservient household roles.[16] Seductively dressed women in ads aimed at male consumers are some of the most blatant examples of using sex to sell a product. A (21st century!) beer commercial that featured bikini-clad models wrestling in mud lowered standards to new levels.[17] This ad was discontinued not because of a change of standards, but because beer sales remained flat.

Finally, the faith that people put in brands may be misguided, as some brands may be overrated or their effectiveness oversold. Consider the following story. Many years ago, a young high school student worked in a Rexall drugstore. The pharmacist/store owner attempted to persuade him to give customers Rexall aspirin whenever they simply asked for aspirin. The pharmacist showed his employee the ingredients listed on the bottles of several competing brands. They were all identical. In addition, the Rexall brand was less expensive than all the other brands.

The young store clerk eagerly agreed to demonstrate his salesmanship skills to unsuspecting customers. The facts were always presented concisely and (more or less) eloquently. During the entire summer, not a single bottle of Rexall aspirin was sold. The image of more established brands was too difficult to overcome, despite the fact that one brand could not possibly have been qualitatively superior because all, by definition, were identical in content. By the way, the young store clerk was the author of this book.

Corporate Advertising

Large firms that produce differentiated products advertise extensively. Because of high levels of economic profit, large firms generally have more funds to promote their products than smaller, imperfectly competitive businesses do. The leading U.S. advertisers include such industry behemoths as Procter & Gamble, Phillip Morris, General Motors, Time Warner, Disney, Daimler-Chrysler, PepsiCo, and Johnson & Johnson. All of these firms are corporate giants by any measure.

Motivated by greater market share and larger profits, large firms seek to inspire brand loyalty. If you think you see many of the same commercials over and over, you do![18] TV Guide has reported that during a single month, Burger King ads were shown on national network and cable TV nearly 5,000 times. In that same month, McDonald's ads appeared over 3,600 times, 1-800-COLLECT ads nearly 2,800 times, and Geico Auto Insurance commercials over 2,500 times.[19]

The establishment of brand loyalty is an important aspect in repeat ads. Not surprisingly, the most popular brand names in the world are[20] McDonald's, Coca-Cola, Disney, Kodak, Sony, Gillette, Mercedes-Benz, Levi's, and Microsoft. Brand loyalty gives these firms and others a significant amount of market power. The more profit they make from consumer allegiance, the more they are able to advertise. As the cycle continues, advertising may become a barrier to entry.

New firms simply cannot afford the huge advertising costs necessary to compete with established firms. Consumers ultimately may enjoy fewer benefits of competition and be faced with only the choices given them by the handful of successful firms.

A classic example exists in the breakfast cereal industry where the four largest companies (Kellogg, General

Mills, Post, and Ralston) advertise heavily. One estimate is that these firms spend about thirteen cents of each dollar of sales on advertising. Profit rates for these four firms have consistently been well above average for companies engaged in manufacturing. Their market shares have also risen. These results have been achieved through successful advertising campaigns.

If either a new entrant or one of the smaller firms in the industry introduced a new product, the big four could stifle the effort by running numerous prime-time TV ads pushing their own brands. These well-established entities offer so many nominally different brands, packaging styles, and other gimmicks that there is little room for a newcomer. When huge advertising war chests create barriers to entry, it is the consumer who suffers.

Neither consumers nor sellers benefit when advertising is retaliatory and self-canceling. The cola wars are a prime example. Two firms dominate the soft drink industry: Coca-Cola Company, with just under half the market, and PepsiCo, with about one-third. The third largest firm is Cadbury Schweppes, with only about a 15 percent market share.

The two leading firms occasionally engage in price wars but their advertising budgets are huge. Both promote their products during major televised athletic events and other TV specials, both use highly visible athletes and movie stars, and both primarily sell hype in ads whose informational content is nonexistent. Consumers ultimately foot the bill for this excess while learning little or nothing about the products. There is little evidence that either firm has substantially gained market share at the expense of the other as the direct result of advertising.

In 1998, PepsiCo acquired Tropicana, the world's leading seller of orange juice, from Canadian liquor magnate, Seagram Co. The move was widely seen as an effort by

PepsiCo to compete more effectively with Coca-Cola Co. In addition to being the world's largest beverage maker, Coca-Cola Co. owns Minute Maid. The battlefield for the cola wars now includes the breakfast table.

There is some evidence that consumers are beginning to fight back against excessive ad creep by large corporations. Government and many firms themselves have been forced to respond. Although the major target has been pop-up ads on Web browsers, others include telemarketers' calls, TV ads to school classrooms, and ads that deface public property such as sidewalks and traffic signals.

Leading the charge has been Commercial Alert, a Portland, Oregon–based consumer awareness group founded by Ralph Nader and Gary Ruskin. The largest number of pop-up ads, which Web users despise but which marketers say bring results, are provided by firms such as X10 Wireless Technology, Orbitz, Providian Financial Corporation, Dell Computer, Bonzi Software, Morgan Stanley, and Columbia House.

In November of 2002, America Online and Microsoft's MSN, the nation's then top two Internet service providers (ISPs), announced that they would take stronger stances against pop-up ads. EarthLink, the number-three ISP, had announced free pop-up blocker software for its subscribers three months earlier. Then popular search engines Google and Ask Jeeves were the first to outlaw pop-up ads on their sites.

The Federal Trade Commission (FTC) created a national no-call list aimed at stopping telemarketer calls, which peaked at 19 million per month in late 2002.[21] Several states have pioneered no-call lists that enable consumers to delete their telephone numbers from telemarketer rosters. The effectiveness of such efforts has been quite limited.

In response to public pressure, Cable News Network (CNN) deleted advertising from its Student News program, broadcast in classrooms nationwide. Various state boards of education have recommended that school districts no longer show the Channel One satellite TV network in classrooms. Twenty percent of its airtime once consisted of commercials. In New York City, Microsoft pasted hundreds of its MSN butterfly logo decals on public sidewalks and traffic signals. Nike similarly trashed sidewalks with its decals. Both firms were forced to remove their handiwork and offer public apologies.

Implications

So where do the various arguments, pro and con, leave us? Many people believe that advertising mirrors American society as a whole, a concept that, if even partially true, is fairly frightening. What we see in the mirror at times is not exactly flattering. Others believe that in order to compete for the short attention spans of those seeking to be entertained, advertising must closely parallel what is seen in movies and on television. There is much truth to this claim. Today advertising, movies, and TV are all long on special effects (technological gimmicks), long on blatant sexual themes, short on acting skills, and long on simplistic storylines. Advertising may sell products for some firms but its usefulness as a source of information to consumers is increasingly being questioned.

Instead of relying exclusively or even primarily on TV and newspaper ads, many consumers, of course, seek objective information from others who have already tried the product. *Trip Advisor*, *Yelp*, and other online sources of customer feedback are becoming increasingly popular. *Consumer Reports* magazine, which for many years has tested products according to various objective criteria, remains popular in its current electronic version.

Ads continue to place some amount of name

recognition in the mind of the potential consumer. This remains a major objective of CEOs and their "publicity engineers". In the meantime, the social usefulness of advertising controversy continues as ads become more technologically sophisticated and genuine informational content has all but vanished.

Veblen foresaw that corporations would eventually create a marketing race that would continuously expand in its scope, thereby becoming increasingly costly.[22] In his view, salesmanship was a wasteful expense, the cost of which would ultimately be borne by the common man. He argued that, since most advertising conveys little or no information, it provides a disservice to consumers. Veblen accurately predicted that selling costs would absorb a rising percentage of the total cost of production over time. As a result, consumers would be cajoled into paying higher and higher prices that had little or nothing to do with production costs. Yet, it is in the latter area where actual qualitative improvement of products might actually occur.

Footnotes:

1. For a summary of these arguments, see: Yunjae Cheong, Federico de Gregorio, and Kihan Kim, "Advertising Spending Efficiency Among Top U. S. Advertisers From 1985 to 2012: Overspending or Smart Managing?" *Journal of Advertising*, 43, 4 (2014), pp. 344-358; Michael R. Baye and Jon P. Nelson, eds., *Advertising and Differentiated Products,* (New York: Elsevier Science, 2001); and Francis X. Callahan, "Advertising and Profits, 1969–1978," *Journal of Advertising Research,* 22, 2 (April–May 1982), pp. 165–169.

2. Hao Li and Hui-Yi Lo, "Do You Recognize Its Brand? The Effectiveness of Online In-Stream Video Advertisements", *Journal of Advertising*, 44, 3 (2015), pp. 208-218.

3. Ryan Hamilton and Alexander Chernev, "Low Prices Are Just the Beginning: Price Image in Retail Management", *Journal of Marketing*, 77, 6 (November 2013), pp. 1-20; Robert L. Steiner, "Does Advertising Lower Consumer Prices?" *Journal of Marketing,* 37, 4 (October 1973), pp. 456–466; and Joseph E. Pluta, "Economies of Scale and Advertising Effectiveness," in Ralph T. Burns and Gerald W. Stone, eds., *Great Ideas for Teaching Economics,* (Glenview, IL: Scott Foresman and Company, 1995), pp. 286–287.

4. Robert B. Eklund and David Scott Saurman, *Advertising and the Market Process,* (San Francisco: Pacific Research Institute for Public Policy, 1988). See also Joseph E. Pluta and James F. Willis, *The Elusive Quest for Efficiency in an Inefficient World,* (Redding, CA: CAT Publishing Company, 2005), especially pp. 244–245.

5. Cornelia Pechmann and Gabriel Esteban, "Persuasion Processes Associated with Direct Comparative and Noncomparative Advertising and Implications for Advertising Effectiveness," *Journal of Consumer Psychology,* 2, 4 (1993), pp. 403–432.

6. Maria B. Royne and Marian Levy, "Reaching Consumers Through Effective Health Messages: A Public Health Imperative", *Journal of Advertising*, 44, 2 (2015), pp. 85-87. A number of worthwhile articles appear in this special issue on health care advertising.

7. Peter Miskell, "Cavity Protection or Cosmetic Perfection? Innovation and Marketing of Toothpaste Brands in the United States and Western Europe, 1955–1985," *Business History Review,* 78, 1 (Spring 2004), pp. 29–60.

8. Kineta Hung, "Why Celebrity Sells: A Dual Entertainment

Path Model of Brand Endorsement", *Journal of Advertising*, 43, 2 (2014), pp. 155-166.

9. Roland Marchand, *Advertising the American Dream: Making Way for Modernity, 1920–1940,* (Berkeley: University of California Press, 1985).

10. John Kenneth Galbraith, *The Essential Galbraith,* (Boston: Houghton Mifflin, 2001) and Naomi Klein, *No Logo,* (New York: Picador USA: 2002).

11. Pluta and Willis, p. 247.

12. Joseph E. Pluta, "Industry Life Cycle Characteristics and Advertising Strategy in a Tight Knit Oligopoly: The Case of the U.S. Brewing Industry," *Southern Business and Economic Journal,* 13, 2 (April 1989), pp.125–141.

13. Gary B. Wilcox, Eun Yeon Kang, and Lindsay A. Chilek, "Beer, Wine, or Spirits? Advertising's Impact on Four Decades of Category Sales", *International Journal of Advertising*, 34, 4 (2015), pp. 641-657. Sales increases did occur but were the result of increases in the alcohol consuming demographic (people between the ages of 18 and 34), tax breaks for producers, and the rise in consumer incomes.

14. Bryan Gibson, "An Introduction to the Controversy over Tobacco," *Journal of Social Issues,* 53, 1 (Spring 1997), pp. 3–11.

15. Elizabeth A. Saylor, Katherine A. Vittes, and Susan B. Sorenson, "Firearm Advertising: Product Depiction in Consumer Gun Magazines," *Evaluation Review,* 28, 4 (October 2004), pp. 420–433.

16. Linda Tuncay Zayer and Catherine A. Coleman, "Advertising Professionals' Perceptions of the Impact of Gender Portrayals on Men and Women: A Question of Ethics?" *Journal of Advertising*, 44, 3 (2015), pp. 1-12; Chun-Tuan Chang and Chien-Hung Tseng, "Can Sex Sell Bread?" *International Journal of Advertising*, 32, 4 (2013), pp. 559-585; and Tom Reichert, "The Prevalence of Sexual Imagery in Ads Targeted to Young Adults," *Journal of Consumer Affairs,* 37, 4 (Winter 2003), pp. 403–412.

17. *The Globe and Mail, Canada's National Newspaper,* (June 20, 2003), p. B7.

18. Susanne Schmidt and Martin Elsend, "Advertising Repetition: A Meta-Analysis on Effective Frequency in Advertising", *Journal of Advertising*, 44, 4 (2015), pp. 415-448.

19. Joseph E. Pluta, *Human Progress Amid Resistance to Change,* (Victoria, British Columbia: Friesen Press, 2010), p. 293.

20. Joseph E. Pluta, "Does Advertising Benefit or Mislead Consumers?" *Perspectives in Business,* 4, 1 (Winter 2007), p. 20.

21. Pluta, *Perspectives in Business,* p. 21.

22. For somewhat different interpretations of Veblen's views on advertising, see: David A. Reisman, *The Social Economics of Thorstein Veblen*, (Cheltenham, UK: Edward Elgar, 2012) and Michael Dawson, *The Consumer Trap: Big Business Marketing in American Life*, (Urbana-Champaign, IL: University of Illinois Press, 2003).

Chapter Ten

Evolutionary Theories of Business Enterprise

I hope we shall crush in its birth the aristocracy of our moneyed corporations which dare already to challenge our government to a trial by strength and bid defiance to the laws of our country.

Thomas Jefferson

The thief or swindler who has gained great wealth by his delinquency has a better chance than the small thief of escaping the rigorous penalty of the law.

Thorstein Veblen

Rather than justice for all, we are evolving into a system of justice for those who can afford it. We have banks that are not only too big to fail but too big to be held accountable.

Joseph Stiglitz

We must guard against the acquisition of unwarranted influence, whether sought or unsought, by the military industrial complex.

Dwight D. Eisenhower

As recently as the late 1990s, any list of the most-successful and most-respected corporations in America would have included names like Enron, Arthur Andersen, JPMorgan Chase, World Com, Adelphia, Tyco, and Martha Stewart. By 2002, the CEOs and other top executives of several of these firms were taken into custody and handcuffed like common criminals. A number of these and other corporate giants were featured in news stories charging fraud, deceptive accounting practices, insider trading, obstruction of justice, and shredding of documents. By 2007, many of these CEOs and their underlings were convicted and were doing, or had done, time in federal prisons. As it turned out, this was just the tip of the iceberg.

In 2008, major banks and insurance companies were exposed for dubious behavior that created the greatest global economic crisis since the Great Depression. Numerous loans to borrowers with inadequate collateral resulted in thousands of mortgage foreclosures and hundreds of companies who quickly found themselves holding loan packages that were little more than worthless pieces of paper. Some firms such as Lehman Brothers quickly exited the scene while others (Bank of America and Chase, to name two of the largest) were labeled "too big to fail" and, after crawling to the federal government for help, were given multi-billion dollar bailout loans.

One insurance company (AIG) received over $100 billion in federal bailout money and then used portions of it to finance bonuses for many of their top executives (some of whom were also treated to luxurious weekend getaways at taxpayer expense) who drove the company to the brink of collapse. Several banks made similar use of government bailout money in a blatant display of arrogance and indifference toward their customers. Incompetently managed auto companies, General Motors and Chrysler, saw their CEOs fly to Washington in corporate jets to beg for government handouts without any plan for restructuring their companies so that solvency might be attained.

A culture of corporate greed has surfaced as excessive executive pay, weak leadership, complacent boards, corrupt analysts, and shockingly fraudulent accounting schemes have been exposed. Numerous corporate executives have broken laws, shaded the truth, and lined their own pockets with huge stock-option profits while stockholders have endured gigantic losses and employees have lost their life savings, their pensions, their jobs, and everything they have spent a lifetime working to achieve.

A number of corporate criminals in these firms have accomplished what Al Qaeda, ISIS, and other terrorist groups have only dreamed: the destruction of billions (!) of dollars of wealth earned by honest, hard-working Americans who believe in the market system and have staked their future on its success. The actions of these corporate lawbreakers have shattered public trust, given American capitalism itself a black eye, and followed a pattern predicted by Thorstein Veblen more than a century ago.

This chapter addresses various ways economists have attempted to account for and model strategic behavior in the world of big business. Despite recent mind-boggling corporate practices and similar behavior for more than 130 years, many Americans still cling to the hope that the vast majority of large firms do, in fact, conduct their business affairs both legally and ethically. Many do. A number of current CEOs and their top assistants bring to their pursuits credentials that include honesty along with business acumen. Nevertheless, while this survey describes patterns in corporate decision making, it also addresses a burning question: Is there something inherent in giant corporate structures that makes them more prone to disreputable behavior?

The Trend Toward Concentration

On the surface at least, corporate leaders have been praised as heroes at various points in American history. The 1920s, 1950s, and 1980s were three such periods. Led by entrepreneurs who delivered products that previously were only dreams of the most optimistic of visionaries, large U.S. corporations offered consumers automobiles, radio, television, jet travel, computers, and a host of household gadgets that made their lives not only more bearable but even pleasant. Competition from Europe and Japan eventually challenged U.S. innovative supremacy, but the end result was a higher standard of living in all of these regions, as well as in several other emerging economies.

One result of this rush to deliver the most advanced of technological wonders was huge shifts in market shares. Dominant among world auto producers just after World War II, General Motors saw its 46 percent market share in 1976 fall to under 25 percent by 2010. Foreign competition, especially from Japan, produced this result. Due to both merger and internal growth, many U.S. industries became highly concentrated. Today, four large manufacturers produce 99 percent of tobacco products made in the United States. The four largest breakfast cereal firms make about 80 percent of ready-to-eat cereals. The four largest airlines carry 70 percent of all passengers. There is even high concentration in the music industry. The top four producers of CDs (Universal/ Polygram, Sony, Time-Warner, and EMI) account for 74 percent of sales.[1]

Many U.S. industries, therefore, are dominated by a small number of very large firms. Economists use the term oligopoly to describe this wide variety of industries which are not monopolies but have substantial market power. In the discipline of political science, an *oligarchy* is a form of government in which people are governed by a select few. *Oligopoly,* a word of similar Greek origin, refers to a market structure in which there are only a few sellers.

Much of basic U.S. manufacturing activity fits the oligopoly model. So does food processing, the automobile and steel industries, aluminum producers, brewers, soft drink manufacturers, airlines, and long distance telephone service. Other examples of oligopoly include the industries that produce household appliances, greeting cards, cameras, soap, lawn equipment, electric light bulbs, motorcycles, coffee, tires, televisions, radios, and men's slacks. Oligopoly, therefore, describes the world of the large corporation whose role in both the U.S. and global economies is extremely important.

Mainstream Oligopoly Models

Numerous mainstream oligopoly models exist and all build on the concept of *mutual interdependence*, which means that what one firm does will often generate a response from rival firms. The most popular of these models today is *game theory*, a form of strategy that involves decision making under conditions of uncertainty, similar to a game of poker or chess.

Other mainstream models include the cartel, dominant firm price leadership, price rigidity, and cost-plus pricing. A *cartel* is a formal written agreement that divides the market and fixes prices. Although illegal in interstate commerce within the U.S., two prominent examples include the Organization of Petroleum Exporting Countries (OPEC) and professional sports. The latter is exempt from antitrust prohibitions due to an absurdly reasoned Supreme Court decision in the 1920s which ruled that sports constituted entertainment and was not a big business.

When a cartel is formed, the result is the same as pure monopoly, at least as long as all firms abide by the agreed-upon rules. From the standpoint of society as a whole, the result is less output, higher prices, a distortion in the allocation of resources, inefficiency, and a tendency for firms to be deceptive with each other. The unimpressive history of cartels includes the dubious character of professional and amateur sports, the electrical equipment industry scandals of the 1950s, the price-fixing convictions in agricultural research in the late 1990s, the political soap opera of OPEC, and other tales of rule bending, fraud, and deception.

In other oligopolies, patterns of implicit collusion, such as *price leadership by a dominant firm*, arise. Compared to competitive industries, inefficiencies occur, prices are artificially high, behind the scenes behavior of questionable legality is commonplace and, worst of all, few incentives for innovation exist. The history of the steel and automobile industries documents these shortcomings. Once again, consumers suffer.

In yet other cases, no dominant firm emerges and the presence of a few roughly equal sized firms may elicit some hope for genuine competition. This is the case of *price rigidity* represented by the kinked demand curve. However, inefficiency again persists, the industry may become sluggish, prices are inflexible, firm output is unresponsive to changes in demand, little incentive to innovate is present, and collusion becomes likely as firms seek cooperation in the face of uncertainty. The airline industry, perhaps the best example of kinked demand curve behavior, has teetered on the brink of collapse long before the terrorist attacks of 2001.

Cost-plus pricing where, instead of setting MR = MC, firms set P = ATC + target profit at normal capacity output, also results in uncompetitively high prices and tendencies toward collusion. This model may come closest to describing how actual firms set prices. Much oligopoly advertising, instead of being informative, contains messages of doubtful value to anyone, drives up prices to consumers, counters and therefore cancels the advertising of rivals, and creates anticompetitive barriers to entry.

In all of these models, mutual interdependence makes pricing according to some static rule, like maximizing profit where MR = MC, somewhat *less* likely. In all cases, the tendency toward some type of formal or informal collusion becomes *more* likely. And yet, none of these models provide insight into the illegal and otherwise dubious behavior that has so dominated the world of the giant corporation.

Three Evolutionary Perspectives

For more than a century, evolutionary economists have had much to say about the inadequacy of mainstream models in explaining corporate behavior. Presented here are three views: those of Thorstein Veblen, Kenneth Boulding, and John Kenneth Galbraith.

Veblen's Theory of Business Enterprise

In 1904, Veblen published his second major work, *The Theory of Business Enterprise.* Not only did this book appear nearly three decades before Edward Chamberlin and Joan Robinson published their theories on monopolistic/imperfect competition, but it also predated all current theories of oligopoly. More importantly, evolutionary economists argue that Veblen's theory of business enterprise is more relevant and more insightful in explaining contemporary corporate behavior than any existing mainstream oligopoly model. During the past two decades, there has been a renewed interest in Veblen's approach, no doubt in part because of recent corporate scandals and the total absence of mainstream explanations as to why they occur.

Veblen did not build formal market structures similar to the models of monopoly or oligopoly. He did, however, conceive of modern American business enterprise as an evolving process from a period of free competition in the eighteenth century to an era of trusts and giant corporations by the late nineteenth and early twentieth centuries. When free competition prevailed, government regulation of business was virtually nonexistent. Because firms were fairly small, bargaining power was rather evenly spread among sellers who produced goods, employees who could still exhibit some amount of creativity in their work, middlemen who transported goods to final destinations, and consumers.[2]

Producer/sellers used their own financial resources, since lending activities of banks were not yet well developed. These entrepreneurs also engaged in considerable price competition by reducing costs and selling larger quantities whenever possible. When technological advances in manufacturing inevitably occurred, costs were lowered further, competition was enhanced, and prices fell along with profits.

Many manufacturing processes required large amounts of technologically advanced capital goods. Only larger firms with substantial financial resources could attempt these investments. The industrial corporation logically evolved and borrowed huge sums of money through issuing securities (stocks and bonds) and obtaining loans from banks, which were growing in size and becoming quite eager to help finance these promising large ventures. Smaller firms that produced fairly standard goods gradually gave way to the new behemoths that began marketing a wide array of diverse offerings to both domestic and foreign buyers. Having emerged in the mid-nineteenth century, this new form of business organization became dominant as the century drew to a close.

Although he acknowledged that such huge injections of new technology greatly increased potential productivity, Veblen saw the corporation as created by borrowed money and ultimately valued on the basis of its presumed earning capacity. Stocks, for example, were continually changing in value. When stock prices rose, the dollar value of the corporation's assets also rose, at least on paper. Buying more machinery on credit further inflated stock prices as the enterprise was perceived to be increasingly healthy. Anticipated earning capacity often drove stock prices to previously unexpected levels. *Saleability* of both the product and the company image began to take precedence over product quality itself. Put somewhat differently, salesmanship began to replace workmanship.

Veblen also saw the personal relationship between producer-sellers and their consumers vanishing because of increasing *absentee ownership*. The corporation was, and is, nominally owned by its stockholders who make fewer and fewer business decisions for the firm. These decisions are made instead by corporate managers. Unlike smaller firms where owner and manager were the same person who was always on site, the owners of corporations were absent from day-to-day operations and relegated executive decisions to professional managers. Rather than maximizing profit, managers of giant corporations became more interested in maximizing the value of the firm's common stock. Higher stock prices are appreciated by shareholders, but so is profitability, which contributes directly to dividends. Goals of managers (captains of industry) and stockholders (absentee owners), therefore, did not necessarily coincide.

Neither did the goals of management and the goals of the community at large, including consumers of the firm's products. Veblen believed that the manager pursuing his/her self-interest generally conflicted with community preferences for efficiently produced goods. Managerial manipulation of stock prices was risky to the health of large firms but not especially dangerous to managers themselves, who held limited amounts of the firm's stock and had the best advanced warning of when it might tank.[3] Further, financial data could sometimes be cleverly manipulated and massaged by the captains of finance to make conditions look better than they actually were. To ensure growth, acquisitions and mergers were pursued with a vengeance. When firms grew in this manner, their earnings expectations generally rose, along with the value of their stock.

According to Veblen, the primary goal pursued in modern corporations is the creation of a stream of revenue. This may come from actually producing goods, from various types of financial manipulation (such as acquisitions and borrowing to inflate stock prices), or from industrial sabotage (restricting output and raising prices). To modern captains of finance, it is immaterial which of these three strategies is used.[4] In the late nineteenth century, cutthroat competition and price wars resulted in many corporate failures. In response, a key strategy eventually became the elimination of these costly price wars which had devastating effects on corporate profits.

To assure the steady flow of desired revenue, Veblen saw corporations resorting to two possible approaches.[5] The first was encouraging yet further types of conspicuous consumption through advertising. There was a limit to how far consumers could be persuaded to behave in this manner, however, and Veblen recognized this fact. In particular, he saw that this partial remedy was unlikely to stimulate firms operating with idle capacity to utilize fully their existing space.[6]

The second approach held greater potential and involved eliminating cutthroat competition through the formation of cartels and trusts. In this way, industrial sabotage could be achieved most effectively as competing giant firms would now restrict output and raise prices *together* while avoiding price wars, special sales, and competing forms of investment. Through trusts and collusion, competitors evolved into collaborators.[7] The winners were the giant firms; the losers were consumers and any pretense of a concept called competition.

In Veblen's view, neoclassical economists oversimplified (and therefore erred in) their analysis by assuming that corporate executives, like all other people in business, always pursued ways to expand output, improve efficiency, and maximize profit for the firm. Instead, Veblen maintained, the modern corporation often exhibited a predatory side that subverted these traditionally assumed goals to achieve financial gain for a few at the top of the corporate hierarchy.[8]

The enormous salaries received by CEOs and other top executives may even be seen in some cases as part of an arranged payoff whereby large stockholders can capture billions of dollars fairly quickly as stock prices are temporarily driven upward by mergers, acquisitions, bank loans, and other expansionary efforts. Those on the inside of the arrangement are likely quite aware that the long-term effects of these manipulative strategies may prove devastating to the health of the enterprise and, therefore, its employees. The insiders, however, are protected from severe loss as long as they sell their stock options before the crisis begins.[9] Their handsome salaries, of course, also help. The negative publicity and even loss of their positions may be a fairly small price to pay if the financial gain achieved during the upswing was large enough.

So long as regulatory constraints are few or are laxly enforced, this process may occur across several industries more than merely a few times. When the day of reckoning inevitably arrives, loyal employees who were not privy to the inside information (outsiders) lose their jobs, pensions, and life savings, while insiders have safely escaped serious financial (and in some cases even legal) consequences. Some even remain on company payrolls of the very firms they helped to dismember.

Recall that in the era of free competition, government involvement in business affairs was limited, in fact virtually nonexistent. Veblen saw government, however, as playing a crucial role in the era of giant corporations largely by intervening *on their behalf.* Veblen viewed a U.S. economy composed primarily of three sectors: finance, industry, and agriculture. Stock exchanges and banks[10] were examples of the first, a number of established industries made up the second, while farms of various sizes accounted for the third.[11]

Within industry, Veblen saw two major market settings. The first was basically what would one day come to be called the dominant-firm price leadership version of oligopoly, where huge corporations dominated a number of firms in the competitive fringe. The second consisted of a large number of small and medium sized firms where no one was dominant and competition, therefore, still took place on a roughly equal footing.

In the first market setting, Veblen envisioned a key role to be played by government, *which was controlled largely by corporate giants to further their own interests.*[12] A pro-business foreign policy[13] including military adventures abroad protected corporate owned property in other countries. Fringe firms in the first market setting and many owners of small and medium sized businesses in the second were fairly easily persuaded to support this role for government on grounds of protecting private property and business interests generally.

Even with this partnership between government and selected corporate conspirators, along with the absence of strict legal supervision, prosperity for a given large corporation eventually ends. Wages and prices of raw materials rise as both resources experience increased demand. This drives up costs and squeezes profits from below. Advances in technology force prices downward and squeeze profits from above. Instead of being sudden, the end is gradual as the firm behaves recklessly and continues to speculate despite falling profits.[14] The long-term effect on the overall economy, as well as on scores of individual families, is potentially devastating.

Parallels between Veblen's description of Gilded Age corporate excess and early twenty first-century scandals involving Enron, Arthur Andersen, Chase Bank, Tyco, AIG and others are concisely summarized as follows:

> As Veblen's theories demonstrated a century ago, these corporate meltdowns, resulting from

> unwise paper acquisitions, mergers, expansions, new stock issues, excessive borrowing, and executive over compensation, all designed to drive up share prices and eliminate competitors, are key ingredients in the current recession. Bankruptcies, precipitous declines in share prices, forced liquidations, major banking losses, and, of course, huge employee layoffs by the mismanaged corporations all helped to fuel the current economic crisis.[15]

The changing nature of business enterprise is indeed a dynamic process which is arguably more accurately captured by Veblen's description than by formal mainstream models. In Veblenian terms, the corporate crises both in his day and at the beginning of the twenty-first century were caused by the acquisitive drive dominating the instinct of workmanship.[16] In the technology versus institutions paradigm, workmanship is a positive force that stimulates the development of technology while the acquisitive drive is a predatory institution which has the capacity to slow economic progress. In seeking short-term pecuniary (financial) gain over long-term productivity, captains of finance lined their own pockets while destroying the firms they (mis)managed, inflicted irreparable harm on their employees and legitimate (mainly smaller) shareholders, and planted the seeds of a downward spiral in the overall economy. As Veblen might have said, two of the longest surviving imbecile institutions are that segment of the corporate system that allows these excesses and abuses to occur and mainstream economics that offers an apology for this behavior.

During the 1920s, Veblen went on to suggest that the forces this evolutionary process set in motion could conceivably lead to a continuing downward spiral and significant economic turmoil.[17] Many scholars see in his forecast an alternative explanation of the roots of the Great Depression which would paralyze global capitalism in the following decade. This is not meant to imply such a scenario would likely repeat itself today because, as evolutionary economists argue, each historical situation is unique with a logically unpredictable outcome. Similarities in the two time periods, however, suggest anything but a positive future development if the initial disturbance is left to run its course.

Given this sobering assessment, is there reason for optimism or pessimism about the future? The discouraging view has two components. The first is that efforts at reform come slowly and reluctantly. Stock options remain at the center of controversy. "(T)heir treatment in corporate accounting are something most neutral financial analysts regard as one of the main culprits in the current accounting and executive compensation scandals. . . . options encourage executives to try to increase short-term profits in order to increase the value of their options, at the expense of long-term growth and stability."[18] A comprehensive review of stock options and other forms of executive compensation is long overdue and would likely contribute much to understanding how creative financing schemes add to the abuse of power.[19] Even these arguments, however, provide an incomplete picture because there are accounting advantages to corporations at present that "the vested interests" are reluctant to disturb:

> The claim in favor of stock options is that they provide incentives for corporate executives to do well because their own fortunes are tied to those of the corporations they run. Less often mentioned is that stock options provide a cheap way of rewarding executives "off the books" because the options do not have to be

> treated as a corporate expense. But stock options generally have the effect of watering down the value of other shareholders' claims and can be used to overstate earnings when not treated as an expense. . . . This failure to count them as an expense inflates the book earnings of the corporation and can give a false impression of the corporation's profitability and financial health. They are, nonetheless, a liability for the corporation. The failure to expense them may serve to drive up the price of the stock and make the options more valuable. So far, the various lobbying groups opposed to changes in the use of stock options have had extraordinary success, and the corporate reform measures debated in Congress . . . (have) not mention(ed) stock options.[20]

The second discouraging component is that even those modest efforts at reform that have been attempted have been largely unsuccessful. To quote one observer, "each new reform seems to bring with it some new distortion, as savvy executives and their lawyers find new ways to bend the rules. . . . They have a strong incentive to do so, for they are rewarded handsomely by their boards of directors and even by their stockholders if they are successful in increasing the market price of the stock. To do this they must play the game of financial expansion, according to the dictates . . . described by Veblen."[21]

Perhaps the major (the lone?) reason for optimism is that many economists and the general public have both become fed up with traditional (mainstream) explanations that either justify corporate chicanery, label specific instances as minor exceptions to otherwise stellar behavior, or ignore the issue entirely. More people are beginning to realize the problem is more prevalent than the few cases that make headlines.[22]

The loyal, hard-working employees of firms like Enron, Arthur Andersen, and numerous other corporate criminals today have nothing to show for their efforts, while various accomplices in ("alleged") illegal activity have either quietly retired to a life of luxury or busied themselves in less high profile occupations. Only in rare and extreme cases do jail sentences occur. To address the problem, an interdisciplinary evolutionary approach appears to hold greater promise in identifying its critical dimensions than any mainstream oligopoly model.

The Boulding Critique

Religious humanist, peace activist, and rogue economist Kenneth Boulding (1910–1993) has argued that potential threats to survival of the firm play a greater role in motivating managerial behavior than profit maximization.[23] Put somewhat differently, fear of loss inspires managers more than hope of gain. This view is consistent with biological evolution, which emphasizes the ability of organisms to adapt to unpredictable changes.[24] Boulding was similarly critical of game theory, believing it could lead to illusions of certainty about the future.[25] Once again, adaptability to unexpected change was considered to be more important than creating artificial expectations of minimal uncertainty.

Boulding rejected marginal productivity theory as an inadequate explanation of income distribution. He did not believe in a movement of prices toward a long-run equilibrium. He did, however, appreciate the harsh realities of diseconomies of scale and, therefore, did not trust large organizations, including corporations and socialist economic systems. He actually saw the two as quite similar, at least in terms of their inefficiency compared to smaller businesses in producing goods at low cost. In his view, both large corporations and socialist governments were bureaucratic dinosaurs. In other words, Boulding held great respect for those businesses that delivered goods efficiently but felt that many corporations were incapable of doing so.

Not only was Boulding critical of oligopoly performance, but he also questioned the ability of neoclassical economics to describe the industrial enterprise accurately. Instead of beginning production analysis with inputs like land, labor, and capital, Boulding believed the important inputs were knowhow (information), matter, and energy.[26] He rejected the labor theory of value (championed by Smith, Ricardo, and Marx) and argued that goods were not produced by labor but by human knowledge (knowhow), operating through institutions that enable this knowhow to capture energy and rearrange materials. In Boulding's evolutionary view, the history of human civilization has involved a succession of short-run equilibria, each of which is undermined by the cumulative, irreversible processes to which they must adapt.

Because of his interdisciplinary interests, Boulding founded a movement that uses "systems analysis" in an attempt to unify the social and natural sciences by seeking propositions that are valid in two or more disciplines.[27] The goal is better communication among specialists such as environmental economists, physical chemists, and water resource engineers. Instead of organizing knowledge and research along the lines of existing fragmented disciplines, Boulding proposed that professionals use the tools of their specialty to study common phenomena such as populations, growth, information, or the interaction between an individual and the environment. He also was a pioneer in peace research and the study of conflict resolution. Many of his diverse interests are surveyed in his 1968 collection of articles titled

Beyond Economics: Essays on Society, Religion, and Ethics.[28]

Boulding's environmental concerns caused him to challenge the basic proposition that all economic growth was beneficial. Instead of the blind, reckless pursuit of consumption without limit, he cautioned that continued pollution of the environment and eventual exhaustion of natural resources would reduce, not increase, living standards. As an alternative to the *cowboy economy*, he substituted the term *spaceship earth* to suggest that we do not live on a mammoth prairie whose resources can be exploited indefinitely but, rather, on a finite planet or enclosed sphere where environmental disaster is possible.

Ever-increasing growth and infinitely expanding consumption, both of which are considered positive outcomes in neoclassical microeconomics, are not possible in a finite world. When limited resources run out, a day of reckoning inevitably arrives. Boulding was optimistic that the necessary adjustments could be made but warned that neither mainstream economic thinking nor traditional corporate behavior would likely be helpful. In his own words, "Anyone who believes exponential growth can go on forever in a finite world is either a madman or an economist."[29]

Large amounts of production and consumption are generally regarded as measures of economic success. Boulding proposed a different economic indicator: maintenance of a given capital stock. By this he meant not only the quantity and quality of physical capital (i.e., goods used to produce necessary consumer goods) but also the quantity and quality of human capital (i.e., human capabilities). Preoccupation with *flows* of goods and services has drawn attention away from maintaining sufficient *stocks* of what is needed to meet human needs. According to Boulding, relatively small, efficient producers are better able to achieve this goal than giant industrial enterprises whose very existence is based on the principle of growth.

The Galbraith Thesis

One of the most prominent economists of the twentieth century, John Kenneth Galbraith has presented an even more powerful attack against oligopoly and the large corporation.[30] In a landmark book entitled *The New Industrial State* and in subsequent writings, Galbraith has argued that, instead of producing what consumers want, large corporations have the power to create and manipulate consumer demand. Threatened by the uncertainty of future demand changes, large firms engage in long-term planning to stabilize demand. Their major vehicle is huge advertising expenses to sell what they can profitably produce instead of what consumers want to buy. Such promotional efforts reduce the risk of innovative new products spoiling the market for existing goods. As a result, *producer sovereignty has replaced consumer sovereignty.*

In addition, according to this view, corporations minimize government interference in their activities by co-opting or corrupting government agencies that possess the legal authority to regulate corporate excess. Instead of serving the public interest, government has become the servant of the corporation. Through its huge political contributions, large and powerful firms are able to undermine public institutions from regulatory agencies to universities. Government, as a result, supplies corporate America with workers educated in its image, funds research that large firms deem too risky, responds with tax breaks and subsidies as needed, and initiates tariffs and import quotas to protect U.S. firms from foreign competition.

Galbraith argues further that separation of ownership and control has created a ruling elite capable of furthering its own interests over those of the public and manipulating federal domestic as well as foreign policy. Large corporations are theoretically owned by their stockholders, who make fewer and fewer decisions about corporate strategy. Those decisions are now made by technically trained managers who are part of an increasingly powerful *technostructure.* This elite group is able to use large corporate profits to further its own agenda over that of a diverse group of investors, as long as those stockholders remain satisfied with an adequate rate of return.

More seriously, Galbraith charges, these industrial technocrats join forces with the military to form a *military-industrial complex*. In this joint effort, corporate managers jump between private sector jobs and prestigious positions in government, where they help make policies beneficial to corporate interests. Such policies include the waging of war to protect corporate investments abroad and lax enforcement of environmental regulations to enhance corporate profits at home.

This devastating critique of corporate America has many advocates and much evidence to support its major arguments. Corporate power is significant by any measure. One writer, for example, proposes several measures of corporate power, the two most workable of which are: (1) the percentage of total government revenue derived from taxes on corporate profits; and (2) the percentage of the labor force that is unionized. When either declines, corporate power increases. Both have fallen dramatically since the 1950s, the first by more than half.[31]

The separation of ownership and control is a fact whose consequences have not always been beneficial to either investors or consumers. Corporate research teams do invent gadgets that advertisers then try to convince consumers will make their lives more complete. Highly profitable corporations are major campaign contributors who obviously expect and receive government favors in return. Former corporate executives turned government policy makers have played key roles in American military ventures in the Middle

East and elsewhere, as well as in a wide range of domestic programs, including some that have harmed the environment.

Critics counter that even the most powerful of corporations have not been sheltered from market forces and changing consumer tastes. Most leading American firms a century ago no longer exist. Many others have struggled to survive and are less influential than they once were. Horse-drawn carriage manufacturers have disappeared, critics argue, because consumers *prefer* automobiles. While such arguments state the obvious, they conveniently ignore the fact that many established large firms remained on the scene longer than they would have in a more open competitive environment.

Even critics admit that advertising influences consumer demand. Most, however, place more faith in the informational value of advertising than recent ads deliver. Critics also point out that, despite government efforts on behalf of business, government also has limited corporate power in several instances. A key example is government warnings about the hazards of cigarette smoking and restrictions on tobacco company advertising, despite political contributions from the tobacco industry. Such arguments downplay the lengthy struggle that was required to eventually win government support for such positions versus how quickly and easily corporations win government favor with its giant payoffs.

An even weaker critique is that, in addition to the influence of big business, government also receives contributions from labor unions, farmers groups, consumer groups, and small businesses. In the halls of government, money talks, and corporations still have more of it than anyone else.

Especially in light of the corporate scandals in the energy, banking, and accounting industries early in the twenty-first century, the Galbraith thesis has become a particularly perceptive corporate critique. The collusion, corruption, incentives to cheat, fraud, and inefficiency so evident in contemporary corporate America stand in sharp contrast to the record of smaller competitive firms in delivering goods consumers want at reasonable prices.

The Pattern of Recent Events

So much of what has happened in the corporate world in recent years can be explained far more accurately by analyses rooted in the tradition of Veblen and Galbraith than by any mainstream oligopoly model. The latter primarily point out a tendency toward collusion before stopping short of further explanation other than litigation which always seems to be several steps behind the next round of corporate aggressiveness. There is so much more that needs to be addressed. One particularly insightful view has recently been offered:

> An economic system that facilitates the privatisation of gains in the hands of ever smaller elites while also socialising risk (losses) in an anarchic manner to the detriment of the many, is not politically viable in the long run. This is the case, in particular, if a core element of this system's legitimacy is its claim to promote democracy at home and around the world, based on principles of transparency and accountability. Both the global financial crisis and the Deepwater Horizon oil spill have already attained the status of 'watershed' events mainly because the social, economic and environmental risks inflicted by private actors on very large groups of people were extraordinary and the causes of failure to manage these risks were systemic rather than accidental.[32]

Put bluntly, banking conglomerates have become even bigger

after the most recent wave of mergers. These giant firms are capable of earning higher profits than smaller banks because they can assume greater risks due to an "implicit bailout guarantee" funded by unwilling taxpayers. Some of these "ordinary citizens" have lost retirement savings due to corporate mismanagement of their accounts. Others have even lost their jobs or means of livelihood. In effect, it is organized and systematized robbery without the use of a gun.

The most asinine argument for federal bailout is the "too big to fail" cliché and the most ridiculous federal policy is bailout of these behemoths which inevitably makes them even bigger. When they cause the next financial crisis just a few years down the road, the cliché will again be recited despite few if any guarantees the first round of money found its way into channels that might have fixed, or at least addressed, the initial problem.

Federal dollars that end up as corporate bonuses to inept executives responsible for the crisis in the first place instead of as loans to consumers potentially capable of investing in new small business ventures are infinitely less productive than dollars given to thousands of impoverished public assistance recipients. Federal money given, or even loaned, to corporations that then increase investment but outsource jobs does little or nothing to alleviate unemployment problems. The stimulus value of such dollars is quite small while the distribution of income becomes increasingly skewed. Any call for government assistance to the new ranks of the jobless is met with its traditional scorn.

It appears reasonable that, in the interest of a more competitive environment, huge banks be broken up into smaller entities, much as government did with AT&T in the early 1980s. Equally logical would be the re-separation of commercial and investment banking.[33]

The first of these would enhance, and in some cases simply create, competition that would benefit consumers, eliminate the "too big to fail"[34] nonsense, and reduce the need for huge federal bailouts in the future. Further, it would encourage more responsible lending practices, internalize risks to the banks themselves, and reduce both the economic and political power currently wielded by megabanks. Alleged economies of scale in banking have proven to be overstated. The benefits of size are clearly smaller than the potential costs large banks impose on the public.

The second of these was initially enacted because banks played the stock market with the money of depositors during the 1920s. Such speculation contributed to the Great Crash of 1929 and the more than decade long depression that followed. Repealing the 1933 law that separated commercial and investment banking was arguably one of the most shortsighted appeals to special interests this country has ever seen.

If commercial and investment banking are again separated, commercial banks could return to the "boring and simple" tasks of accepting deposits and making standard loans. Under this proposal, bailout of gambling casino institutions like investment banks would be strictly prohibited. In the free market, such firms would be free to succeed or fail. Those that became profitable would attract additional clients while those that lost money would exit from the industry. Sadly, because of the strength of the "vested interests", neither proposal is likely to be undertaken any time soon.

Pressure to deregulate financial markets in the last two decades of the 20th century recreated an only slightly modernized version of pre-Great Depression banking.[35] For those who had learned from history, chaotic results were predictable. Imagine what might have happened if social security had been privatized before 2007, as many in the financial sector had hoped. Enormous fortunes would have morphed into the hands of unscrupulous money managers while most Americans would have seen their retirement savings stolen from them.

The experience of JPMorgan Chase Bank is most instructive. After "allegedly" underwriting a substantial portion of the Enron financial scam and paying $2.2 billion to avoid prosecution of the charge,[36] the bank has consistently been involved in lawsuits claiming fraud, racial discrimination in lending practices, and numerous other charges.[37] When federal bailout money came its way, some of the cash was awarded as bonuses to top executives and mergers have made the firm more powerful than ever. Chase routinely contributes to the political campaigns of those who sit on prestigious Congressional banking committees. Is the competitive invisible hand of the marketplace working effectively in the Chase case?

Despite repeated instances of corporate misbehavior, the view somehow persists that unregulated megafirms will automatically produce results that are both ethical and beneficial to all.[38] Until that view disappears[39] or is at least substantially modified, repeated financial crises, each successive one more severe in magnitude, are highly plausible.

Footnotes:

1. Joseph E. Pluta, *Small Trees in the Large Forest,* (Redding, CA: CAT Publishing, 2006), Ch. 7.

2. Tuna Baskoy, "Thorstein Veblen's Theory of Business Competition," *Journal of Economic Issues,* 37, 4 (December 2003), p. 1124.

3. William T. Ganley, "The Theory of Business Enterprise and Veblen's Neglected Theory of Corporation Finance," *Journal of Economic Issues,* 38, 2 (June 2004), p. 399. See also Lino Sau, "Instability and Crisis in Financial Complex Systems",

Review of Political Economy, 25, 3 (July 2013), pp. 496-511 and Cristina Peicuti, "Securitization and the Subprime Mortgage Crisis", *Journal of Post Keynesian Economics*, 35, 3 (April 2013), pp. 443-456.

4. James V. Cornehls, "Veblen's Theory of Finance Capitalism and Contemporary Corporate America," *Journal of Economic Issues,* 38, 1 (March 2004), pp. 29–58, especially p. 34. See also Jeremy Green and Colin Hay, "Towards a New Political Economy of the Crisis: Getting What Went Wrong Right", *New Political Economy*, 20, 3 (2015), pp. 331-341 and Malcolm Sawyer, "What is Financialization?" *International Journal of Political Economy*, 42, 4 (2013), pp. 5-18.

5. Baskoy, pp. 1128–1129.

6. Thorstein Veblen, *The Theory of Business Enterprise,* (New York: Charles Scribners Sons, 1904), p. 255.

7. Thorstein Veblen, *The Engineers and the Price System,* (New York: Viking Press, 1921), p. 127 quoted in Baskoy, p. 1129. See also Kees Van Der Pijl and Yuliya Yurchenko, "Neoliberal Retrenchment of North Atlantic Capital: From Corporate Self-Regulation to State Capture", *New Political Economy*, 20, 4 (2015), pp. 495-517 and William Redmond, "Evolution of Corporate Governance Principles Among U. S. Firms", *Journal of Economic Issues*, 44, 3 (2010), pp. 615-627.

8. Veblen, 1904, p. 20. See also Cornehls, p. 35. The overall movement of the economy toward financial concerns has recently been described in Tae-Hee Jo and John F. Henry, "The Business Enterprise in an Age of Money Market Capitalism", *Journal of Economic Issues*, 49, 1 (March 2015), pp. 23-46.

9. Antoon Spithoven and Piet Keizer, "Markets and Rules: The Case of the Global Credit Crunch", *Journal of Economic Issues*, 45, 2 (June 2011), pp. 391-400. See also Donald C. Wellington and Sourushe Zandvakili, "Globalization and Inequality According to Veblen," *International Journal of Social Economics,* 31, 11/12, (2004), pp. 1061–1070.

10. J. Patrick Raines and Charles G. Leathers, "Veblenian Stock Markets and the Efficient Markets Hypothesis," *Journal of Post Keynesian Economics,* 19, 1 (Fall 1996), pp. 137–151 and J. Patrick Raines and Charles G. Leathers, "Financial Innovations and Veblen's Theory of Financial Markets," *Journal of Economic Issues,* 26, 2 (June 1992), pp. 433–440.

11. Baskoy, p. 1130.

12. Baskoy, pp. 1130–1131.

13. Joseph E. Pluta and Charles G. Leathers, "Veblen and Modern Radical Economics," *Journal of Economic Issues,* 12, 1 (March 1978), pp. 129–130.

14. Veblen, 1904, pp. 195–196, as quoted in Baskoy, p. 1131.

15. Cornehls, p. 43.

16. Philip Anthony O'Hara, "The Contemporary Relevance of Thorstein Veblen's Institutional-Evolutionary Political Economy," *History of Economics Review,* 35 (Winter 2002), p. 92.

17. Veblen, *Absentee Ownership and Business Enterprise in Recent Times,* (New York: B. W. Heubsch, 1923), pp. 418–445.

18. Cornehls, pp. 47–48.

19. Irwin M. Stelzer, "The Corporate Scandals and American Capitalism," *The Public Interest,* no. 154, (Winter 2004), pp. 19-31; John Vickers, "Abuse of Market Power," *Economic Journal,* 115, 504 (June 2005), pp. 244–261; Stephen M. Renas and Richard J. Cebula, "Enron, Herding, and the Deterrent Effect of Disclosure of Improprieties," *American Journal of Economics and Sociology,* 64, 3 (July 2005), pp. 743–757; and Joseph E. Pluta, "Evolutionary Economic Explanations of Corporate Scandals", *Perspectives in Business* 5, 2 (Fall 2008), pp. 23-29.

20. Cornehls, p. 48; Brian J. Hall and Kevin J. Murphy, "The Trouble With Stock Options", *Journal of Economic Perspectives*, 17, 3 (Summer 2003), pp. 49-70; Marianne Bertrand and Sendhil Mullainathan, "Are CEOs Paid for Luck? The Ones Without Principals Are", *Quarterly Journal of Economics,* 116, 3 (August 2001), pp. 901-932; and John Abowd and David Kaplan, "Executive Compensation: Six Questions That Need Answering", *Journal of Economic Perspectives*, 13, 4 (Fall 1999), pp. 145-168.

21. Cornehls, p. 45.

22. John Grahl, "The Professors and the Banks: U. S. Views on the Subprime Crisis", *International Review of Applied Economics*, 28, 3 (May 2014), pp. 383-400; Brian Fahey, "A Critical Review of Neoclassical Modeling Techniques in Structured Finance", *Journal of Post Keynesian Economics*, 35, 3 (April 2013), pp. 319-340; and A. Larry Elliot and Richard J. Schroth, *How Companies Lie: Why Enron Is Just the Tip of the Iceberg,* (New York: Crown Business, 2002).

23. Kenneth E. Boulding, *The Organizational Revolution: A*

Study in the Ethics of Economic Organization, (New York: Harper, 1953).

24. Kenneth E. Boulding, *Evolutionary Economics,* (Beverly Hills, CA: Sage Publications, 1981) and Vladislav Valentinov, "Kenneth Boulding's Theories of Evolutionary Economics and Organizational Change: A Reconstruction", *Journal of Economic Issues*, 49, 1 (March 2015), pp. 71-88.

25. Kenneth E. Boulding, "Social Risk, Political Uncertainty, and the Legitimacy of Private Profit," in R. H. Howard, ed., *Risk and Regulated Firms,* (East Lansing: Michigan State University Graduate School of Business Administration, 1973).

26. Robert Waters, "What Happened to Boulding's Evolutionary Economics?" *Journal of Economic Issues,* 40, 2 (June 2006), pp. 465–471.

27. Joseph E. Pluta, "Kenneth Boulding's Skeleton of Science and Contemporary General Systems Theory", in Wilfred Dolfsma and Stefan Kesting (eds.), *Interdisciplinary Economics: Kenneth E. Boulding's Engagement in the Sciences*, (London: Routledge, 2013), pp. 48-60.

28. Kenneth E. Boulding, *Beyond Economics: Essays in Society, Religion, and Ethics,* (Ann Arbor: University of Michigan Press, 1968).

29. Quoted in R. P. Beilock, *Beasts, Ballads, and Bouldingisms: A Collection of Writings by Kenneth E. Boulding,* (New Brunswick, New Jersey: Transaction Books, 1980).

30. For a concise collection of Galbraith's most important

arguments, see John Kenneth Galbraith, *The Essential Galbraith,* (Boston: Houghton Mifflin, 2001). For a recent summary of many of Galbraith's positions, see Steven P. Dunn and Stephen Pressman, "The Economic Contributions of John Kenneth Galbraith," *Review of Political Economy,* 17, 2 (April 2005), pp. 161–209.

31. Randy R. Grant, "Measuring Corporate Power: Assessing the Options," *Journal of Economic Issues,* 31, 2 (June 1997), pp. 453–460.

32. Stephanie Blankenburg, Dan Plesch, and Frank Wilkinson, "Limited Liability and the Modern Corporation in Theory and in Practice", *Cambridge Journal of Economics*, 34, 5 (September 2010), pp. 821-836.

33. Both of these proposals as well as several others are made by Helge Peukert, "The Financial Crisis: Origins and Remedies in a Critical Institutionalist Perspective", *Journal of Economic Issues*, 44, 3 (September 2010), pp. 830-838.

34. Andrew Ross Sorkin, *Too Big to Fail*, (New York: Viking Press, 2009).

35. William Van Lear and James Sisk, "Financial Crisis and Economic Stability: A Comparison Between Finance Capitalism and Money Manager Capitalism", *Journal of Economic Issues*, 44, 3 (September 2010), pp. 779-793.

36. Joseph E. Pluta, "The Role of Chase Bank in the Enron Scandal", in Daniel Fireside and Amy Gluckman, *Real World Banking and Finance*, 6th ed., (Boston: Economic Affairs Bureau, 2010).

37. Joseph E. Pluta, "Chase: A Bank for the New Century?",

Dollars and Sense, No. 270, (Spring 2007), pp. 24-27, 35.

38. Joseph E. Pluta, "The Libertarian Fantasy of an Ethical Market", *Research in the History of Economic Thought and Methodology*, 25-A, (2007), pp. 13-23.

39. William K. Black, *The Best Way to Rob a Bank is to Own One,* (Austin, TX: University of Texas Press, 2005).

Chapter Eleven

Institutionalism and Government

When they call the roll in the Senate, the Senators do not know whether to answer 'Present' or 'Not Guilty'.

Theodore Roosevelt

You want a friend in Washington? Get a dog.

Harry Truman

A system cannot fail those it was never meant to protect.

W. E. B. Du Bois

By the power elite, we refer to those political, economic, and military circles which, as an intricate set of overlapping cliques, share decisions having at least national consequences.

C. Wright Mills

Congress voted for tougher laws on corporations. So now when a corporation buys a senator, they need a receipt.

Jay Leno

Mainstream analysis of the economic role of government has generally centered on such issues as taxation, tariffs, subsidies, rent controls, price supports, price floors, tax credits, minimum wage laws, regulation, antitrust, merger policy, macroeconomic effects of fiscal policy, and the use of benefit/cost analysis to evaluate government programs. Market failure is generally seen as providing the microeconomic rationale for government intervention in private markets. Such failure occurs because of *externalities*, which are spillovers or neighborhood effects (positive or negative) that are not captured by market supply and demand curves.

Private goods are characterized by the exclusion and rivalry principles. The *exclusion principle* states that everyone is excluded from the benefits of a good except the person who pays for it. The *rivalry principle* states that one person's consumption of a good prevents someone else from consuming that good. Public goods like national defense, lighthouses, and sunsets are not subject to either exclusion or rivalry.

Whenever spillover benefits or positive externalities exist, the market underallocates resources. Whenever spillover costs or negative externalities exist, the market overallocates resources. Government subsidizes spillover benefits and penalizes (taxes) spillover costs in an effort to achieve a more socially optimal quantity of output.[1] Government may be unable to correct for market failure in every circumstance. This fact is especially evident when one considers that government frequently tackles problems that the private sector has already failed to solve.

Provision of public goods is hampered by the *free rider problem*, or tendency of people to avoid paying for the benefits of a good when it can be obtained free. Since people are often unwilling to reveal their true preferences for public goods, such goods may be underproduced by private markets. Government should not always do what the private sector cannot do efficiently. If (marginal) costs are quite high and (marginal) benefits very low, it may be better if government does not intervene.

Application of microeconomic principles to public sector decision making may at first appear difficult because of problems in measuring government output and because government agencies are not driven by the profit motive. In *benefit/cost analysis*, net benefit, calculated as total benefit minus total cost, is used as a proxy for profit. As long as benefits can be measured in dollar terms, the private sector decision rule may be adapted for public sector decisions as follows: maximize net benefits by setting marginal benefit equal to marginal cost.

The *present value discounting formula* presents future dollars in terms of present dollars or, in other words, reverses the compound interest process. Present value analysis is often necessary in benefit/cost studies because both benefits and costs flow unevenly over time. *Cost/effectiveness analysis* is a special case of benefit/cost analysis used when benefits cannot be measured in dollar terms. Proxy measures of effectiveness, which approximate benefit in non-dollar terms but which are clearly quantifiable, are used in such analyses. If specific goals are established, outputs are measured instead of inputs, valid indicators are used, and weighted multiple proxies are employed instead of single measures, cost/effectiveness analysis, despite its shortcomings, can generally assist public sector decision making.

An Eclectic Evolutionary View

On the issue of the appropriate role for government in the economy, most schools of thought are rather specific, if not dogmatic. Because institutionalism is a dissent against neoclassical economics, and since the latter advocates minimal government involvement, it might be tempting to conclude that the evolutionary approach advocates a definitive or specific type of government action in given circumstances. This, however, is not an accurate inference.

Institutionalists are not of one mind on the extent of government participation in the economy. Most economists in this school would agree that, in solving problems, it is correct to be experimental and that, if experimentation proves effective, such policies should be implemented. This is one of the ways in which the philosophy of pragmatism has influenced the school. If a strategy has a proven track record (if it works), then it would be foolish not to employ the means of getting to the desired end. If a government program, therefore, can accomplish what the private sector cannot, then a rigidly ideological antigovernment stance would be impractical.

According to the mainstream perspective, markets are strictly private. The market and government, in other words, are separate and distinct spheres of activity. On occasion, the mainstream view continues, government interferes in private markets. It is clear from historical evidence, however, that government action in private markets is frequent and pervasive. The mainstream conceptualization, therefore, is inaccurate.

Many evolutionary economists, on the other hand, emphasize that markets are not private but public institutions, brought into existence by and maintained through government oversight.[2] These exchange institutions would not exist, nor would they be able to continue evolving, were it not for the collective action that established and molded them over many decades. In other words, a market is an accumulation of working rules to settle issues involving exchange.

Of course, these exchange institutions are for the private exchange activities of natural and legal persons. However, they are products of collective action and would break down in the absence of such action due to the continuous flow of disputes that arise in exchange transactions. In the view of evolutionary economists, therefore, a market is a public institution established and maintained through sovereign collective action to facilitate private exchange. When well designed and well maintained, markets minimize external costs encountered in private exchanges.

Some History

Veblen himself was skeptical that the institution of government was up to the challenge of correcting the market failures he observed. Many of his students and followers, however, became actively involved in President Franklin Roosevelt's New Deal, the federal program that tackled the problem of widespread unemployment during the 1930s.[3] As discussed earlier, noted institutional economist John R. Commons played a considerable role in encouraging an active state government approach to public utility regulation. He and several others also felt strongly that government could be helpful in a number of other areas. For many reasons, therefore, institutionalism has come to be associated with a reform mentality.

Classical and neoclassical economics were seriously discredited by their generally laissez faire stances in dealing with the Great Depression. By contrast, any approach willing to engage in experimentation attracted listeners during this difficult time. Many historians of economic thought consider the 1920s and 1930s to represent the apex of institutionalist influence on the economics profession. Despite the overall positive performance of the economy during the Roaring 20s, Veblen was being heard by those who questioned the large amount of speculation as well as the financial irregularities of the time. His warnings about the potential for impending economic disaster proved to be accurate, although he died just weeks before the stock market crash of 1929.

Those of his followers who served in FDR's New Deal, including selected members of the president's newly formed Brain Trust, brought a prestige to the economics profession that had previously been lacking. Institutionalists helped to define a new role for economists as advisors to presidents in the policy area. Since the Brain Trust was the forerunner of the formal Council of Economic Advisors, which was established in 1946 and which exerts important influence on federal policy to this day, professional economists owe much to selected institutionalists and others in opening the doors of government to their expertise. After World War II, a growing number of state and local governments followed suit in seeking the advice of professional economists on a wide range of issues.

Ultimately, however, the macroeconomics of John Maynard Keynes overshadowed the institutionalist contribution. The Keynesian role of government was more explicitly outlined and its policy guidelines were easily adapted to fit the needs of a number of market oriented economies worldwide. Keynes also outlived Veblen by some seventeen years. This gave Keynes the opportunity to influence government policy for a longer period during the troubled years of Depression and war. The pragmatic Roosevelt was not ideologically indebted to the approach of any school of thought. He never met Veblen but did meet Keynes twice. FDR and Keynes, by the way, had little or no respect for each other. Some Keynesian-type ideas, however, were already being implemented by the American president even before Keynes published his famous work in 1936.

The followers of Keynes were more successful than those of Veblen in reconciling their founder's approach with the methods of mainstream economics. (Veblen himself, and many of his disciples, of course, believed that any sort of reconciliation was impossible and undesirable.) The National Bureau of Economic Research, founded by noted institutional economist Wesley C. Mitchell, gathered much of the necessary statistical data on which many Keynesian prescriptions could be based. Although Keynes has been discredited in recent decades, his approach has been more openly debated and more directly attacked by mainstream economists than that of Veblen. Evolutionary economics, as a result, has fallen outside of the boundaries of established dialogue between those who largely accept the neoclassical versus the Keynesian positions.

It should be emphasized that these boundaries have largely been built around *macroeconomic* controversies, given the importance that big-picture issues have assumed since the Great Depression. In attempting to regain respectability, economists in the classical and neoclassical traditions faced a formidable challenge from the followers of Keynes. This occupied much of their thinking for several decades. As the role of government grew in fact (even as this expansion remained controversial), attempts at reconciling or even synthesizing classical and Keynesian approaches dominated discussion. Because specific points of difference still remain, discussion of whether synthesis is possible is ongoing.

Institutional economics, by contrast, primarily challenges the *microeconomic* approach of the mainstream. Given the logic and evidence supporting this challenge, it is difficult to explain why it has not either gained wider acceptance or stimulated more debate within the profession. The mainstream obsession with mental exercises built around mathematically precise, but narrowly structured, formal models has continued in the tradition of the nineteenth century neoclassical search for scientific precision. Institutional resistance to those new ideas that question established economic doctrine may have also played a role. If the discipline is to address more contemporary economic and social problems, it will find it increasingly difficult to downplay the rich and diverse insights of the evolutionary approach.

Benefit/Cost Analysis and Institutionalism

Benefit/cost analysis of government programs may be an important case in point. Evolutionary economists applaud the gathering of empirical evidence to evaluate whether government is doing its job well or poorly. Unlike more esoteric constructions built around marginal utility or a purely competitive ideal, the measurement of benefits and costs holds some promise as one of the more potentially useful applications of neoclassical principles. Benefit/cost analysis addresses the critical question of just what it is that a specific program is attempting to do. As a result, it can provide practical information for decision makers.

Evolutionary economists, however, would qualify these assertions with several cautions. They would, of course, insist that a wide range of possible methods and goals be considered. Benefit/cost analysis naturally is interdisciplinary in scope and must include more than just economic variables. There is nothing inherent in its method that prevents it from being holistic or confines it to being static. Although it does use maximizing and minimizing techniques, it makes no dubious assumptions about human behavior and need not be rooted in hedonistic psychology.

The role of institutions (government and other) in resisting change is an important, and even critical, component of any benefit/cost analysis. So long as caution is exercised in the measures chosen and analysis is not limited only to that which is measurable, meaningful results may be obtained.[4] Directly addressing such pressing issues as education, health care, and the environment is a focus long overdue in the economics profession.

The biggest problem inherent in benefit/cost analysis concerns the distribution of benefits and costs. Who gets most of the benefits and who pays most of the costs? All too often, this question is ignored, and it does make a difference, sometimes an enormous one. A benefit-cost analysis, for example, may provide justification for building a high-speed rail system between the downtown areas of two major cities. Benefits accrue primarily to those who work in, do business in, live in, or visit the two metropolitan areas. Substantial costs, however, are borne by those living in the rural and smaller urban areas that lie between the two major destination points. Farms may be split, small communities may lose business, housing values may plunge, noise pollution may be considerable, and other negative results may occur. Evolutionary economists would insist that the analysis is invalid, and certainly incomplete, unless a thorough accounting of who is affected and by how much is given in each case. These more thorough, wide-ranging effects cannot possibly be captured by a single benefit/cost ratio.

The problem is more serious and may even be insurmountable in cases of a military effort or pollution control program, where effects on human life are most important and impossible to measure. American weapons manufacturers, their CEOs, and their stockholders benefit handsomely from military ventures, while an incalculable cost is borne by the families and friends of those soldiers who die in battle. A toxic waste disposal facility generates benefits by supposedly minimizing harmful effects of toxins. Many of these effects, however, are unknown, deceptively downplayed, and likely incomprehensible for some time into the future. Those low-income and minority families located closest to such a site are most likely to experience the negative externalities more quickly than others.

The evolutionary economist advises against the overselling of incomplete benefit/cost analyses that neglect or minimize the human side effects of programs popular among vested interest groups. On one hand, exclusive reliance on those factors which are measurable, for example, commits the error that is commonplace in mainstream analytics. On the other hand, a benefit/cost format that is holistic, eclectic, dynamic, and humane holds promise as an aid to decision makers. Noneconomic and difficult to measure variables along with institutional resistance to change clearly must be addressed. Decisions based on partial information cannot possibly be better than those which take into account a more complete tally of benefits and costs to all affected by a proposed government action.

Governmental institutions merit especially close scrutiny. Laws, of course, are subject to varying interpretations by the courts. Congress and state legislatures may adopt attitudes toward specific programs that differ from those supported by benefit/cost studies. Political reasons for doing things are often at odds with economic arguments. The neoclassical assumption of rational economic behavior on the part of politicians and civil servants may be as farfetched, or perhaps even more so, than the alleged rationality of consumers. Close relationships between selected government officials and corporate donors may assure anything but a rational result beneficial to the public interest. For all of these reasons and more, institutional restraints to change must again be given center stage.

Rival agencies unwilling to share information, corruption, inertia, cronyism, and other maladies are all factors that cannot simply be assumed away for the sake of a model, whether benefit/cost or other. Unrelated riders attached to important appropriations bills, preservation of vested interests, and the "you scratch my back and I'll scratch yours" mentality are all part of the government way of doing things in the United States and elsewhere. (It should be mentioned that many of these problems are as common in private business as in government.) All of these institutional matters make objective analysis of many issues difficult and, by definition, less precise than in narrowly constructed benefit/cost models. Institutional economics merely requests that institutional factors be recognized and be given consideration in public sector decision making.

Is There an Institutionalist Theory of Government?

Although several evolutionary economists have written about the role of government in specific instances, a comprehensive institutionalist theory of government has yet to be proposed. Veblen, Galbraith, and many others following their lead have, of course, argued that government intervention tends to support vested interests including large corporations.[5] The use of government in reform-minded activities, including regulation, documents another role government has played. Only a few attempts at formally defining the role of the state from an institutionalist perspective, however, have been made.

A prominent contemporary institutionalist, Charles Leathers,[6] has documented that, in *The Theory of Business Enterprise*, Veblen introduced a theory of government failure based on the delusion possessed by the general citizenry that policies benefiting businesses also were in their best interests. Leathers shows further that this argument is later developed more fully in *The Vested Interests and the Common Man.* Having introduced in the first of these works a theory of political parties and in his writing during World War I the idea that government officials pursue their own self interest, Veblen does not, however, reexamine these issues in his later work. Evolutionary economists, therefore, are left with only incompletely developed suggestions from Veblen on the economic role of government.[7]

Two other contemporary institutionalists, William Dugger and Warren Samuels, offer contrasting but related viewpoints. Dugger[8] sees the state as being both a productive (nurturing) and predatory (exploitive) institution, as possessing a dual nature that offers opportunities while at the same time limits them, and as simultaneously uplifting the poor while defending the rich against the poor. The symbol of its productive side is the welfare state with its message of hope to the downtrodden, with its resources devoted to health care and education, and with its legal framework that historically, however, has favored the corporation over the labor union and the First Nations tribe.

The symbols of its predatory side are its limited room for those at the top and its need to teach discipline, humility, and respect for both property and hard work to those with limited skills. Its resources include defense contracts and other support of selected business ventures while its legal apparatus has protected the corporation at the expense of workers. As a result, the state exercises power and distributes it to selected participants in the economy.

Samuels[9] maintains that whether government plays a large or small role is not as important as who government supports when it does intervene. He also sees government as being both the actor and the one acted upon. The distribution of income and wealth, for example, depends partly on government, while government is partly dependent on the distribution of income and wealth. Unlike classical economics, which primarily views the effect government has on private markets, institutional economists see cause and effect moving in both directions. Government is both a dependent and an independent variable. This interaction, therefore, has important implications for the distribution of power in the economy. It is power that determines whose interests predominate.

A number of institutional economists including Galbraith, Douglas Dowd,[10] and A. Allan Schmid[11] have similarly emphasized that *the question is not so much whether government should intervene but rather on whose side government does intervene.* When courts rule in favor of corporations and against workers, they confer power. When Congress makes laws limiting what rights workers and unions can demand, it confers power. When the executive branch rewards those special interests that helped place it in office, it confers power.

Upon whom power is given by government is a far more pertinent issue than whether the dollar amount of government expenditure is relatively large or small. By focusing on the latter issue along with the alleged inefficiency of government, neoclassical economists and their ideological supporters have drawn attention away from the fact that governmental institutions confer power. How that power is conferred and who gets it versus who does not is a logical place for an institutionalist theory of government to begin.

Noted institutional economist Phillip Klein has directly challenged the neoclassical agenda to downsize government by offering empirical evidence that government in the United States 1) is not growing rapidly, if in fact it is growing at all, and 2) is smaller than in most industrial economies.[12] Klein argues that neoclassical preoccupation with big government masks their larger ideological concerns over which functions (such as domestic social programs and public services) government should perform. He concludes:

> Downsizing is the latest battle cry of those who continue to believe the real world is accurately encompassed by some combination of Say's Law . . . and a laissez faire system featuring flexible wages and prices, widespread voluntary unemployment, and endemic complacency and lethargy among the poor on welfare (combined with no diminution of the vigor of the profit motive among the entrepreneurs deserving tax reductions and accelerated depreciation allowances).[13]

A rather large body of earlier research supports the argument about the size of the U.S. public sector relative to that of other nations[14] and the fact that government in the United States and elsewhere may be getting smaller relative to the size of the economy once inflation is taken into account.[15] Institutional economists are less concerned about the size of government and more concerned about how effective specific government programs are in improving the quality of life, how government regulation serves the public interest, and how government actions confer power on selected groups.

Embraced by institutional economists, one final concept called path dependency may be especially relevant in their analysis of government. *Path dependency,* it will be recalled, is sometimes broadly interpreted as simply meaning that history matters. What has occurred before, perhaps by design but more likely by chance, has set in motion a sequence of events that has followed a given direction or path. A more specific view emphasizes the self-reinforcing nature of institutions. Feedback provided to the existing path often assures that the established path proceeds without modification. A chance experiment, for example, may yield a technology that is used indefinitely without considering other, possibly more efficient, options.

The two most commonly cited examples are the keyboard and the gauge of railroads. Early typewriters began with the sequence of letters Q-W-E-R-T-Y. This placement of letters was designed to eliminate jamming of keys while other letter groupings allowed for faster, more efficient typing. Even though the early mechanical glitches were quickly resolved, the QWERTY set-up remained and was soon reinforced by typing manuals and instruction kits based on this early line-up of letters. Such positive feedbacks enthroned QWERTY as the standard keyboard. Changing from it now would require not only a technological adjustment but also the retraining of millions of users.

On railroads, gauge is simply the distance between the rails. Back in the 1820s, horses pulled metal carts carrying coal and other materials from mines. The rails on which the wheels of these carts rested were built 4 feet, 8 1/2 inches apart. With his typical wit, Veblen noted how these "silly little bobtailed carriages" (still in use in 1915) slowed the development of superior technology by "the restraining dead hand of . . . past achievement."[16] Today, passenger trains that reach nearly 200 mph roll on the exact same gauge of rails. Different gauges have been shown to be more efficient, especially when long railroad cars must negotiate tight curves. Making those changes on millions of miles of track and on millions of existing railroad cars, however, simply is no longer feasible due to the cost involved.

While these and other examples emphasize path dependency due to established technology preferences, similar lock-in may also occur because of long-held behavior patterns.[17] Government policy choices may persist due to arbitrarily set paths long ago. Examples include the traditional way military planning and budgeting has been conducted in the Pentagon bureaucracy for decades and the fact that the major determinant of current budget levels in all federal agencies has long been the previous year's budget.

In the first case, limited results were achieved during the 1960s when the planning programming budgeting (PPB) system forced policy makers to concentrate on outputs rather than inputs and to use benefit/cost analysis. In the second case, zero-base budgeting (ZBB) was largely unsuccessful during the late 1970s in getting agencies to justify their entire budgets from zero rather than using last year's budget as a base.

Behavioral lock-in remains in evidence in an abundance of federal, state, and local programs. Agricultural price supports and subsidies to farmers remain on the path established over seven decades ago, despite their long-documented ineffectiveness. Similar arguments may be made about tariffs designed to protect domestic firms, rent controls in many U.S. cities, and bureaucratic inertia elsewhere.

Much like circular and cumulative causation, the accepted path may be moving toward either a beneficial or harmful outcome. More precisely, insofar as government programs are concerned, the path may be moving toward a beneficial outcome for some but a harmful outcome for others. Farm programs benefit large agricorporations and vote-seeking politicians while harming small farmers and consumers. Tariffs on foreign steel help inefficient domestic producers and American steel workers while hurting efficient foreign producers, American consumers of products made with steel (especially automobiles), and trading patterns generally.

Many government programs today are still implemented according to path dependencies inaugurated when conditions may have justified such patterns but no longer do.[18] Evolutionary economics, with its emphasis on studying past binding institutional resistance to change, appears especially well equipped to focus on needed changes in execution of government programs.

A Final Word

No foolproof approach exists in analyzing such complex government programs as the pursuit of a clean environment, national defense efforts, protection from adverse weather conditions, and various domestic social programs. In these areas, as well as in many others, experimentation is often necessary. If effective, the approach merits continuation and modification over time to adapt to changing circumstances. If ineffective and a program is crucial, another experiment is in order. Rigid ideological stances are generally counterproductive.

Evolutionary economists have provided advice in shaping numerous government programs in the Progressive

Era (1900–1917), the New Deal (the 1930s), the Great Society (1960s), and in other critical periods in U.S. history. Obviously, some of these programs have been more successful than others. When not prohibitively expensive, those that have been effective have accomplished much more than if nothing had been done or if solutions had been left strictly to the private sector.

Benefit/cost analysis works best when it is broadly conceived; when it considers the role played by government institutions including the courts, legislatures, and executives; when it examines the possible effects of corruption and cronyism; and when it accounts for who receives benefits and who pays costs.

Prior to and during World War I, Veblen introduced a theory of market failure and argued that government officials tend to act in their own self interest. In his later writing, however, he did not develop these ideas further and clearly offered no overall model of the conduct and consequences of government activity. Since Veblen's day, a number of evolutionary economists have studied specific public policy issues but a general institutionalist theory of government has yet to be developed.

At times, government appears nurturing when devoting resources to support education and health care. At other times, it protects corporations at the expense of workers and allocates billions to defense contractors for weapons systems that are never used. Tax breaks, subsidies, bailouts, and lax enforcement of both antitrust provisions and environmental laws nurture corporations and harm everyone else including small businesses.

Evolutionary economists maintain that the size of government is less important than who it supports when it does intervene in the economy. *Government institutions confer power.* How that happens, who benefits, and who does not would be a logical focus when an evolutionary theory of government eventually is advanced.

Do specific government programs improve the quality of life for many citizens or merely cater to special interests? Has innovative program design occurred when necessary or has path dependency simply reinforced existing institutions and contributed to inertia? Questions such as these are a major component of evolutionary inquiry. When policy makers take them more seriously than partisan rhetoric, many government programs may receive their first serious scrutiny in decades.

Assessing the effectiveness of government spending and taxation is often difficult but not impossible. In addition to the analytical technique chosen and the quantitative results obtained, what also matters is history, institutions, noneconomic factors, and human acceptance of change.

Footnotes:

1. Mainstream analysis has not exactly rushed to embrace evolutionary principles in its discussion of public expenditure and tax proposals. One recent effort is Luca Micheletto, "Optimal Nonlinear Redistributive Taxation and Public Good Provision in an Economy with Veblen Effects", *Journal of Public Economic Theory*, 13, 1 (February 2011), pp. 71-96.

2. I am grateful to Bill Dugger for his explanation of the market as a public institution.

3. Rick Tilman, "Thorstein Veblen and the New Deal: A Reappraisal," *The Historian*, 50, 2 (February 1988), pp. 155-172. For an interesting study of New Deal institutions, see Jason E. Taylor and Todd C. Neumann, "The Effect of Institutional Regime Change Within the New Deal on Industrial Output and Labor Markets", *Explorations in Economic History*, 50, 4 (October 2013), pp. 582-598.

4. For the most comprehensive work in this area written by an institutional economist, see A. Allan Schmid, *Benefit/Cost Analysis: A Political Economy Approach,* (Boulder, CO: Westview Press, 1989).

5. Tae-Hee Jo, "Saving Private Business Enterprises", *American Journal of Economics and Sociology*, 72, 2 (April 2013), pp. 447-467.

6. Charles G. Leathers, "Thorstein Veblen's Theories of Governmental Failure", *American Journal of Economics and Sociology*, 48, 3 (July 1989), pp. 293-306.

7. Sidney Plotkin and Rick Tilman, *The Political Ideas of Thorstein Veblen*, (New Haven: Yale University Press, 2011), especially pp. 14 and 42.

8. William M. Dugger, "The State: Power and Dichotomy," in Warren J. Samuels (ed.), *Fundamentals of the Economic Role of Government,* (New York: Greenwood Press, 1989), pp. 49–58.

9. Warren J. Samuels, "Some Fundamentals of the Economic Role of Government," in Samuels (ed.), pp. 167–172.

10. Douglas F. Dowd, *U.S. Capitalist Development in the United States Since 1776: Of, By, and For Which People?,* (Armonk, NY: M. E. Sharpe, 1993).

11. A. Allan Schmid, "Economy and State: An Institutionalist Theory of Process and Learning," in Samuels (ed.), pp. 173–178.

12. Phillip A. Klein, "Downsizing Government: Size and Institutionalist Principles," *Journal of Economic Issues,* 36, 2

(June 1997), pp. 595–604.

13. Klein, p. 604.

14. See, for example, Joseph E. Pluta, "Growth and Patterns in U.S. Government Expenditures, 1956–1972," *National Tax Journal,* 27, 1 (March 1974), pp. 71–92 and Joseph E. Pluta, "National Defense and Social Welfare Budget Trends in Ten Nations of Postwar Western Europe," *International Journal of Social Economics,* 5, 1 (1978), pp. 3–21.

15. Morris Beck, "The Expanding Public Sector: Some Contrary Evidence," *National Tax Journal,* 29, 1 (March 1976), pp. 15–21; Joseph E. Pluta, "The Real Growth of the U.S. Public Sector over the Past Half Century," *Southwest Business and Economic Review,* 20, 1 (August 1982), pp. 15–36; Joseph E. Pluta, "Real Public Sector Growth and Decline in Developing Nations," *Public Finance,* 36, 3 (1981), pp. 439–454; and Joseph E. Pluta, "The Declining Public Sector Thesis: An Additional Test and Implications for Developing Regions," *Social and Economic Studies,* 28, 4 (December 1979), pp. 69–84.

16. Thorstein Veblen, *Imperial Germany and the Industrial Revolution,* (New York: Macmillan, 1915), pp. 125–128.

17. William Barnes, Myles Gartland, and Martin Stack, "Old Habits Die Hard: Path Dependency and Behavioral Lock-in," *Journal of Economic Issues,* 38, 2 (June 2004), pp. 371–377.

18. As the following sources indicate, the concept is widely used in several disciplines besides economics. See Raghu Garud, Arun Kumaraswamy, and Peter Karnoe, "Path Dependence or Path Creation?" *Journal of Management Studies*, 47, 2 (June 2010), pp. 760-774; Taylor C. Boas,

"Conceptualizing Continuity and Change: The Composite-Standard Model of Path Dependence", *Journal of Theoretical Politics*, 19, 1 (January 2007), pp. 33-54; and James Mahoney, "Path Dependence in Historical Sociology", *Theory and Society*, 29, 4 (August 2000), pp. 507-548.

www.ingramcontent.com/pod-product-compliance
Lightning Source LLC
Chambersburg PA
CBHW051453170526
45166CB00001B/225

9781519290953